THE GREATEST BUSINESS COACHING BOOK

THE GREATEST BUSINESS COACHING BOOK

A QUANTUM LEAP CATALYST PROCESS

TERRY OSTROWIAK

LitPrime Solutions
East Brunswick Office Evolution
1 Tower Center Boulevard, Ste 1510
East Brunswick, NJ 08816
www.litprime.com
Phone: 1-800-981-9893

© 2025 Terry Ostrowiak. All rights reserved.

No part of this book may be reproduced, stored in a retrieval system, or transmitted by any means without the written permission of the author.

Published by LitPrime Solutions: 05/15/2025

ISBN: 979-8-88703-470-6(sc)
ISBN: 979-8-88703-471-3(hc)
ISBN: 979-8-88703-472-0(e)

Library of Congress Control Number: 2025909850

Any people depicted in stock imagery provided by iStock are models, and such images are being used for illustrative purposes only.

Certain stock imagery © iStock.

Because of the dynamic nature of the Internet, any web addresses or links contained in this book may have changed since publication and may no longer be valid. The views expressed in this work are solely those of the author and do not necessarily reflect the views of the publisher, and the publisher hereby disclaims any responsibility for them.

What business owners are saying about

The Greatest Business Coaching Book...

Terry helped me achieve goals I didn't think were possible. Now I am confident I can increase my revenues by 300%. Thank you Terry!

M.R.

Terry's coaching helped me have a greater belief in my own abilities and realize my true value. This book captures the essence of Terry's Coaching and will forever improve your business and your life.

P.J.

Terry, thank you. You have written an incredible book. I have read many books about business but yours stands out like a beacon. It has empowered and influenced me to take a quantum leap in results. I have been able to "make it rain" and my entire business has benefited. I could not have done this without you. Your book gave me an edge and a huge advantage over my competition. I carry it in my briefcase. I refer to it daily because of its functionality.

It is my handbook.

M.S.

Terry challenged me to follow my dreams. With his guidance I've gone further than I ever thought possible. This book is a must read for every business owner.

P.M.

This really is the best Coaching book ever written. Thanks Terry for addressing the needs of business owners. Now I am thinking about starting my own home-based Coaching business.

J.F.

Many of us spend our lives searching for success when it is usually so close we can reach out and touch it.

RUSSELL H. CONWELL

ABOUT THE AUTHOR

Terry Ostrowiak *is currently the President of Dynamus® International, providing global resources and coaching services to business owners and management. His Quantum Leap Catalyst™ Process consistently achieves extraordinary results and places Terry in a category unto himself. Terry's extensive career as a Coach spans over 40 years and 26 countries. He has organized and conducted coaching and training programs and practical workshops for a wide range of small and large companies.*

For twelve years, Terry ran one of the most successful independent Dale Carnegie operations in the world from his base in Johannesburg, South Africa. He received the much-coveted "International President's Cup" three times for excellence in generating and conducting quality business.

Terry was appointed special advisor to the International Federation of Professional Coaches and Mentors, has hosted his own online radio program and is the Founder and President of Dynamus® *International, a Global Coaching Consultancy.*

Additionally, Terry is a Past-Board Member of the San Diego Branch of The Professional Coaches and Mentors Association.

*The fulfillment of every great
achievement was impossible at first.*

Terry Ostrowiak

Contents

PART I: INTRODUCTION

Chapter 1. Why I Became a Coach 1
Chapter 2. The 'AHA' Moment 13
Chapter 3. What is 'Coaching'? 14
Chapter 4. The Need for Coaching 17

PART II: HOW TO COACH

Chapter 5. Ask for Permission to Coach in a Process of Willing Cooperation 25
Chapter 6. Create a High Level of Trust Between Coach and Client 29
Chapter 7. Set Clear Objectives based on the Client's Needs 32
Chapter 8. Use Profiles as Tools for Improving Communication 35
Chapter 9. Focus on Strengths, Not Weaknesses 41
Chapter 10. Add Energy to the Client's Cause 45
Chapter 11. Instill Confidence in the Client to Reach New Heights 49
Chapter 12. Access Our Intuition – Document the Vision – Create the Plan 52
Chapter 13. Eliminate Doubt and Feelings of Inadequacy ... 56
Chapter 14. Show Genuine Belief in the Client's Ability to Change 60

PART III: THE ELEMENTS OF BUSINESS COACHING

Chapter 15. Start with a Vision not Goals 71
Chapter 16. Listen Actively – Not Passively 75
Chapter 17. Practice Correctly 79
Chapter 18. Be Clear! 83
Chapter 19. Challenge Clients 87
Chapter 20. Clarify Commitment 91
Chapter 21. Adapt to Cultural Differences 94
Chapter 22. Talk 'I Language' not 'You Language' 98
Chapter 23. Believe in Our Ability to Make a Difference ... 101
Chapter 24. Tune-in to Our Inner Voice 104
Chapter 25. Dialogue not just Discussion 108
Chapter 26. Let Action Live on the Tongue 112
Chapter 27. Make it Easy to Do 115
Chapter 28. Create Urgency to Get Things Done 118
Chapter 29. We Learn From Or Failures, but Grow
             From Our Successes 120
Chapter 30. Conclude Each Session by Reinforcing New
             Learning 123
Chapter 31. Heighten Our Awareness of 'The
             Pygmalion Effect' 127
Chapter 32. Live up to High Expectations 133
Chapter 33. Remembering Names 139
Chapter 34. Demonstrating Leadership 144
Chapter 35. Performance Appraisals for Adults 146
Chapter 36. Can You Sleep When the Wind Blows? 149
Chapter 37. Some Life Lessons 151
Chapter 38. AHA Moments List 155

PART I
Introduction

If we want a place in the sun, we have to put up with a few blisters.

ABIGAIL VAN BUREN

1
Why I Became a Coach

It was my first day at school. I was six years old and my teacher was Mrs. Adcock. She was sweet and gentle, rotund and likeable and yet I was still afraid, mainly of the group of other pupils – but for no reason I could think of.

We sat in single desks in long vertical lines – about 30 of us.

At around 11:00 I needed to pee. I could not bring myself to interrupt the class and when it became too much to hold back I let it go. On the floor beneath my desk was nothing less than a swimming pool, becoming bigger and bigger and my misery increased proportionately.

The lesson went on, but I never heard a word. I was far too enveloped in my own thoughts wondering how I was going to wade out of the classroom without embarrassment.

The bell rang. Nobody said a word. They knew as I knew, but from a different perspective.

Even Mrs. Adcock said nothing.

As I walked to the playground the light breeze reminded me

that my new, gray short pants were soaking and I now felt cold as opposed to the warmth that I had felt in the classroom. I buttoned the little gray jacket with the green badge on the breast pocket that my mother had so proudly sewn on that weekend. This garment, to me, was a symbol of my becoming a man. Now it just hid my shame.

One boy pointed at me and excitedly exclaimed as though he had discovered gold, "Look! He wet his pants."

I chased him and tried to hit him with my new gray cap as the flood of embarrassment crept up my neck to my face and almost choked me. He was too fast so I let it go.

After a while the wetness just dried up, but not my feeling of inadequacy. In the subsequent days no one said a word about the incident. I didn't even tell my parents.

At 14 years old, while in high school, I was given a two-hour after school detention by a Latin teacher because I failed to translate a sentence assigned for homework, not because I hadn't studied, but because I could not regurgitate it on demand. I was too flustered to perform under the watchful eyes of the class and the little Napoleonesque Latin teacher.

Although I came from a loving, gentle family and was never physically punished for any wrongdoing this inordinate fear of being embarrassed affected me until I reached adulthood.

Maybe that was the start of my need to be compassionate towards others who lacked confidence – to be a coach to those who were afraid to perform optimally under stress. Later, I realized that I had paid my dues to master my skill. I had

learned to develop a highly sensitive awareness to people in pain and then learned to articulate my insights so that they touched the appropriate nerve endings.

Through school and even at university I felt that most teachers simply went through the motions of teaching rather than really connecting with their students. Maybe it was because they needed to be the focal point themselves, rather than the students.

It was at age 21, one night in the first session of a Dale Carnegie Course, that I once again came face to face with reality. I sat on a table with five other adult class members, in front of an audience of about 35 people. The instructor asked me my name, where I came from and a few other innocuous questions to connect me with the group.

I found myself spluttering the answers with little coherence. I became aware that I had forgotten how to breathe. After each answer I neglected to exhale. After the third question, I felt so self-conscious that the instructor suggested that I take a deep breath and then continue. I did, and as I concluded my talk, he gently complimented me. Although I did not hear exactly what he said, I sensed his support and felt more relaxed as I made my way back to my seat in the group.

Never before had I experienced such a sense of warmth and support in a formal group setting, and at the same time I was aware that I had also stretched myself outside of my normal comfort zone and that I would never be the same again.

I had always wanted to be helpful – particularly to people in need. However I was so frustrated as a Social Work student that I was often emotionally affected by our 'visits of observation' to various institutions. This new experience with positive business people in such a diverse group of adults gave me a totally new perspective. After about eight sessions I mentally decided that this style of 'coaching' was going to play an important role in my life. I concluded that my initial intuition about this style of instruction was correct. **People respond wonderfully to learning conducted in an atmosphere of approval rather than one of criticism.**

A few weeks after the program ended I was invited back to be a graduate assistant. For 14 weeks I was a support assistant to about six of the 40 class members. My commitment was to ensure that each one of my team completed the course successfully. In addition, I supported the course instructor in the running of each session.

Over many years, I performed this volunteer work 29 times – 14 weeks per course and often two courses at a time at night. I started at the age of 21 while still at university and when I was 24 years old the local licensee, Bob Hopkins, invited me to join the organization full-time as a salesperson and promoter of courses.

Being too young to become an instructor, I continued as a graduate assistant at night and gained a huge amount of experience in the business. This was extremely helpful in the growth of my career a few years later.

My first public presentation as a representative of Dale Carnegie, at the age of 24, was a turning point for me and wiped out the years of fear and embarrassment I had felt many times previously in group situations.

The advertisement in the papers drew a huge crowd to the Maria van Riebeeck Hall in downtown Johannesburg.

I had prepared for weeks to do this two-hour demonstration alone and was determined to enroll everyone present in the course. All seven people arrived on time and I did the presentation of my life. It was definitely show-time for me, not for them, but we all survived and I believe we all enjoyed the experience.

This started my 40+ year love affair with Public Speaking, Instruction and Coaching. *Although I have worked in a number of different positions in various organizations during my career, nothing has ever matched the thrill of being a coach to my own instructors, staff and clients in the 26 countries in which I have operated.*

Earl Nightingale

One night after a session on a course in 1964, the instructor asked our group to stay behind and listen to a recording from Earl Nightingale. I was 21 years old at the time and had never heard of Earl Nightingale.

A course leader attached a record player to the wall socket and for the next hour our group listened to the recording. The story was narrated by a deep, mellow voice and was called 'The Strangest Secret'.

It was a spellbinding story and when it concluded we all sat mesmerized as we contemplated the message we had just experienced.

In a nutshell, the message is: **'We become what we think about all day long!'**

With beautiful metaphors and compelling word pictures we literally saw the possibility of a rosy future unfolding before us, and shackles binding us slipped to the ground as we contemplated the offer of freedom that had just been presented to us.

This moment shaped my life as I absorbed the enormity of the possibility before me.

Even then, I had no idea how vitally I would be affected by those words in my life and future career.

This was my first major watershed experience, nowadays called a break-through experience – what I now call an "AHA" moment.

From that moment I started to set goals for my life. I visualized what future would be right for me. I started to literally create pictures in my mind of those things my intuition clicked with and I even briefly wrote down what I visualized. More than anything else I suddenly began to realize that the clearer the picture was for me in my mind, the more easily I could see it becoming a reality. I did not realize at that time that I was constantly reinforcing my intuition and making it concrete.

Almost eleven years later my first important written goal became a reality. I started my first business as CEO. Obviously the picture in my mind influenced the direction I had been taking over the previous years. As I look back now, over 30 years later, it is very clear, but at the time it was simply me working from day to day subconsciously following my dream. To me it was already a strong possibility, then it became a reality and finally a certainty.

The pattern is clear. The clearer we visualize what we want to come true, the easier it is to attain. It is almost as though our subconscious works overtime beneath the conscious level and makes it happen. All we have to do is feed our mind with the right ingredients and eventually the plant will grow as we envisioned.

Not surprisingly, Earl Nightingale is now considered one of the greatest thinkers and inspirational men of our times and recognized for 'The Strangest Secret' – 'We become what we think about'.

From his own enlightenment Earl wrote <u>The Strangest Secret</u> Message. He found irony in that this truth of why we become, whatever it is we become, is no secret at all and he found it most strange that everyone didn't know about it.

Recorded in 1956, the demand for the recording of *The Strangest Secret* grew so large that Earl received a Gold Record – the only record of its kind to receive such an honor. Earl, who passed away in 1989, wrote and recorded more than 7,000 radio programs and his Our *Changing World* became one of the world's most syndicated programs and he was recognized as one of the founding pioneers of the personal development industry.

I was lucky enough to bring Earl to South Africa at one time and we became quite friendly in the last years of his life, meeting and talking regularly. My wife and I still maintain a close relationship with his wife Diana.

During one of our visits to the USA before we moved to San Diego, Earl discussed with me the dilemma many people have with career paths. I asked him how we determine what our purpose in life should be and what guideline we could use to shape our destiny.

He said, "There are some people in the world I call 'River People'.

They have one specific talent that is so glaringly obvious there is no possibility of them doing anything else with their lives other than exploiting their gift to its greatest advantage. Like a river meanders its way through hills, valleys swamps, deserts and the various extreme elements of weather, River People will not be denied as they roll towards fulfilling their destiny regardless of barriers or impediments.

"However, the rest of us who do not have this condition have to find other ways to play out our lives meaningfully. Sometimes we have many competing talents. We therefore have to dig inside, access our intuition, set goals, commit ourselves to follow-through and then unwaveringly stay on track until we attain our objective."

Earl always said, *"Success is the Progressive Realization of a Worthy Ideal. I believe that Success in life depends on focusing on our greatest skills then continuously pursuing new ways of utilizing them so that we are inspired to move towards making our vision a reality."*

Dale Carnegie

I have had a number of mentors over the years who have guided and worked with me, starting with Bob Hopkins who first employed me at Dale Carnegie. He believed in me and gave me a free rein to try whatever I wanted to do with no barriers. This helped me to believe in myself and solidified my self confidence.

Dick Morgal, my original trainer and friend for over three decades, taught me professionalism and discipline without imposing it. He was always supportive and coached me to raise the bar to new heights by setting a wonderful personal example. He was a shining version of a person who lives with integrity as his guiding light.

Duncan Ehlers, also a DC trainer at one time from Buenos Aires, Argentina, and afterwards based in the USA, helped me to develop the Executive Image Program (EIP), promoted by most Dale Carnegie Sponsors around the world. This cooperation with Duncan in Johannesburg was a highlight in my life because his intricate, analytical skills combined with my broad vision and drive resulted in an inspiring partnership and high-level growth for both of us.

This period was the most innovative of my career because we challenged ourselves to create a Program for Executives, not necessarily their subordinates, and simultaneously sell the idea into the Dale Carnegie Organization.

The acceptance of this program as part of the syllabus of the organization was as much a reward in itself as the growth and pleasure that Duncan and I derived from the development process.

I chose to look for opportunities to train new and experienced instructors on the EIP using the same Executive Coaching techniques I had originally developed, rather than make the course the focal point. I therefore inadvertently learned to clearly define the coaching process that would later become the focal point of my career.

This insight enabled me to distinguish between the 'Coaching Process' itself and the content. I soon realized I was 'Process Driven' and not 'Content Driven'. I could apply this coaching technology to any material or situation either with individuals or groups. The 'secret source' was not in the content of the program, but in the process of delivery.

As a result of this insight I spent a number of years in Europe training instructors from Scandinavia, Great Britain, Israel, Iceland, Hong Kong and the Netherlands to reproduce this Technology and to date they have had more success in producing Executive Image Programs than anyone in the USA.

The Netherlands

In February 1987, after selling my Dale Carnegie License, I moved to The Netherlands. My colleague and dear friend Sherman Brown, the licensee for most of the UK had acquired the license for The Netherlands and had run a few courses but needed someone to set up an operation there. He asked me to come over for a year or two and somehow it stretched to 12 years.

A few months after arriving, I managed to create a loose, long-term contract with KMG one of the largest auditing companies in The Netherlands. They had just acquired Peat Marwick and combined the two companies to form KPMG – then the largest accounting company in the world. They had also expanded their operation into management consulting, tax, auditing, electronic data processing, management training and a host of other professional disciplines.

They asked me to conduct some programs for partners to create a common culture between the more conservative Dutch management from KMG and the more liberal American management from Peat Marwick.

This process continued for ten years as I coached and trained over 650 people from senior management through young high-potentials who were starting their careers with the organization.

From this base, working alone in my business, I managed to acquire contracts with some really large Dutch organizations such as KLM Royal Dutch Airlines, DSM Dutch State Mines, The European Space Agency, AKZO NOBEL, ABN AMRO Bank, and ING Bank.

In addition, almost every weekend for years I trained and coached licensees, managers, salespeople and instructors for Dale Carnegie in 25 countries in Europe, Scandinavia and The Middle East.

Finally in 1998, my wife and I moved to the USA to be close to our daughters who were studying in San Diego.

It's kind of fun to do the impossible.

WALT DISNEY

2

The 'AHA' Moment

Have you ever had a moment when 'a light bulb' above your head seemed to go on as we figured out something was either difficult to understand or troubling us? Of course, there is no actual light bulb but researchers have discovered there are times when a surge of electrical activity affects our brain. Often problems that require specific insight can prompt this electrical activity, aptly called AHA moments.

These AHA moments are particularly important in the coaching process both from the client's and coach's perspective. For the client it's the signal – the feedback that acknowledges understanding. It's that 'click of the fingers' with the accompanying realization of 'I get it.'

For the coach, it's a measure of success and something to strive for in every coaching session. **Each coaching session should have at least one AHA moment. Both the coach and the client reap the benefits.**

Many AHA moments are described in the following pages of this book collected from years of actual coaching situations. **And, at the conclusion of each chapter check the AHAs to better understand the coaching process.**

3
What is 'Coaching'?

I am amazed and often distressed to hear how many people, many of them highly professional, call themselves coaches when they simply do not coach – but rather mentor, counsel, instruct, advise, teach or just sell their own ideas or those of their company. It's very confusing!

The definition of coaching is warped and often bent out of shape without insight as to what the profession of coaching demands. Coaching is a specific methodology and process distinctly different from other processes.

Recently I attended a breakfast promotion conducted by a professional marketing specialist who positions his process as one of coaching when it's simply a consulting or mentoring exercise revolving around his material. He was promoting his methodology for improving business systems and the process was essentially consulting using his format and material with some backup instruction.

I am certain he is very successful, but why not present himself honestly as the marketing or business development consultant he is?

A language teacher recently told me she was a coach. On questioning her I discovered that she instructs teachers at schools on how to use the materials and systems sold and marketed by the company she represents. She has never had any training or instruction in coaching and knows nothing about this distinct discipline.

The vital distinction between consulting, mentoring, advising, instructing, and counseling vs. coaching is that the coach serves as a catalyst and focuses only on the client's agenda. The other disciplines are almost solely focused on their own professional agendas.

As the years progressed, I tried to differentiate my role from the plethora of so-called coaches. I see myself as one chemical element, with my client another. In combination, if formulated well, the mix is optimal and the activity is mutually satisfying. A third, more powerful element is created from the relationship. Neither of the first two elements alone could create this result, but together the additional energy that appears is a product of pure synergy and 1+1 can = 3. Synergy comes from combining two words – 'Syn' abbreviated from 'Synchronize' and 'Ergy' from 'Energy'. The product of 'Synchronizing the Energy' between a coach and client often transforms the relationship.

Most coaching is great fun and very rewarding as it is focused on achieving desirable future results. It's like taking a walk with a highly enthusiastic person, discussing them at their very best.

In order to be a good coach, I postpone judgment and see my clients as they could be, at their very best – not necessarily as they are. Somehow I translate this emotionally and physically to them so that they experience a huge feeling of acceptance and safety and become free to discuss with me their deepest anxieties and fears. The feeling of being truly listened to is such an unusual experience for most business people that they often sigh with relief that someone finally understands them. From then on we can focus our dialogue on future vision and goals.

Coaching is not meant to be a long-term process, but rather the right tool for the right moment. The coach needs to know when to let go rather than take the client through a never-ending therapeutic dependency. Coaching then becomes what it was meant to be: an event-driven process, unlike other disciplines such as counseling or providing psychological advice.

AHA Moments...

- Coaching means visualizing people at their very best, rather than as they are now.

- The vital distinction between consulting, mentoring, advising, instructing, and counseling vs. coaching is that the coach serves as a catalyst and focuses only on the client's agenda. Other disciplines are almost solely focused on their own professional agendas.

- Coaching is not meant to be a long-term process, but rather the right tool for the right moment.

4
The Need for Coaching

Today, more than any other time, the need to perform successfully has never been greater. As a result of this solitary focused activity on self we have lost interest in the people who count in our lives. We seem to be constantly focused on our own achievements and struggles to achieve our place in the sun. This leaves little time to be concerned with the needs of others.

As many of my clients say, they have no one to talk to who they can trust – no one to whom they can reveal their innermost secrets, fears, or inadequacies because they do not trust the neutrality or confidentiality of those around them.

This is why I am a coach – because I can do these things and also add my varied background experience to the package.

My job is extremely rewarding as I chide, tease and figuratively poke clients in the ribs in order to challenge them to open themselves to change.

Jean Houston, a leading pioneer in the exploration of human

potential, in an interview with Larry King, asked him to think about the person who had the biggest influence on his broadcasting career, "The person who you modeled yourself on."

He said, "Horace Greeley."

She then said, "Imagine that he was here. Tell him what you most admire about him." So he did.

She then said, "Imagine that you are Horace Greeley. What would surprise you most about broadcasting today?"

She coached him to talk as though he was Horace Greeley giving his impressions of broadcasting today and what had changed.

She then asked him to imagine that Horace Greeley was giving advice to Larry King and coached him to play both roles, which he did.

The result was that Larry King placed himself in the shoes of Horace Greeley and articulated a future vision for himself, which he said he had not previously verbalized. His excitement about this new insight was apparent. His face relaxed and there was a new look of wonder in his shining eyes as he acknowledged the value of the experience. He then commented on Jean Houston's supposed 'séance' with Hillary Clinton that had been raging for weeks in the media. Like the experience with Larry King, she quickly removed the mystery from the controversy. All she had done was to ask the former First Lady some meaningful questions which clarified some gray areas.

This was a superb example of effective coaching rather than the facilitator or counseling approach, often confused with professional coaching.

Recently, the head of resources at a large international company admitted to me that their policy of training all senior management to be coaches had failed. First, most of the participants believed they understood the principles of coaching and could do it without training. Therefore when they were practicing the process they listened with a slightly prejudiced ear. Secondly, they demonstrated they were not adept at listening and mostly missed the cues from the speaker, being more intent on following the tasks they had learned rather than actively listening between the lines.

The result is that even today they believe they are good coaches, but if you ask their subordinates, very little coaching occurs. Mainly, the subordinates have to listen to well-meaning advice from their experienced superiors or watch their managers demonstrate their own skills without ever having an opportunity to test themselves in a real situation with a supportive coach present.

Many managers think that coaching is simply the act of demonstrating their own superiority. Unfortunately, this action almost always produces negative results as students learn how inadequate they are in relation to the prescribed model and end up helplessly watching 'Superman or Superwoman' at work while being exhorted to do the same. Nothing destroys confidence faster than this process and the only solution is to leave and find new environments and an alternative context in which to practice. Meantime the boss says things like: "How disloyal; How ungrateful; I gave them so much training and coaching and they didn't appreciate it!"

I often wonder how many 'high potentials' in businesses leave for greener pastures after tremendous resources were spent on their development. They could have given a marvelous return on investment if they had only been handled in a more professional and insightful manner.

The process of coaching looks easy when viewed from the outside. Like most skills viewed by amateurs, it looks simple to reproduce, but the reality is that it takes inordinate hours of practice to make the implementation appear that simple.

You may say this concept of coaching sounds like it has a large business focus, but the reality is different.

Business owners need to know how to coach their staff and be coached to raise their own potential every bit as urgently as executives need to do so in large businesses. Even more, in a small business each person is so vital to the smooth functioning of the company that if they are dysfunctional or leave unexpectedly their departure leaves huge gaps in the puzzle.

On the other hand, if business owners create an adult-to-adult culture and 'coach' their staff rather than try to 'manage' them, the employees feel, 'this is my business,' like 'my family,' and recognize they can contribute and self-actualize within the company rather than use the experience as a stepping stone to start their own company.

Many years ago, a dear friend of mine from South Dakota, Dr. Jerry Simmons, taught me a life-long lesson. He owned a number of small radio stations in his area and was an outstanding entrepreneur and businessman.

He said, "Terry, when you employ people, tell them right from the *start, 'Stay with me as long as you feel you are growing and any time you feel down or depressed in your job, come and tell me. I need to know what's happening with you and I can't tell how you are all the time, so you need to keep me in the loop.'*

He went on to say, 'Any time you feel you are not growing, come and tell me immediately and we can discuss it. If we can't resolve the situation I will assist you to find a new job outside of our company.'

Wow! What a commitment to his people – and they responded accordingly.

Of course on hearing this philosophy, I implemented it immediately into my business and was able to create a functional, 'humanistic' culture in our company based on 'adult to adult' relationships.

AHA Moments...

- Focus on others' achievements and struggles, not ours – a great way to develop more self-confidence.

- Challenge clients to open themselves to change.

- Create an adult to adult relationship.

- Straight talk with dialogue and deep respect is better than being 'nice' or being 'autocratic.'

PART II
How to Coach

A prudent question is one half of wisdom.

FRANCIS BACON

5

Ask for Permission to Coach in a Process of Willing Cooperation

Nothing is more irritating or annoying than people who offer advice without asking for permission to do so. And I mean genuinely asking and checking that the listener is truly willing to listen to what they have to say and acknowledges the request.

I have a friend who is an experienced golfer and often tells me what I'm doing wrong *after* I've hit a bad shot on the course. I know that he's trying to be helpful and is probably seeking recognition for his high standard of skill.

However, every time he comments, he forces me back into focusing on a previous negative experience while I'm trying to concentrate on playing the next shot perfectly. If he said: "This time try to watch the back of the ball until you have struck it," I would be more amenable to his suggestion. His comment is in the present and I have the choice to try something new or reject it.

Very few people understand the subtle nuances in coaching

until they have experienced being coached by a skilled professional. They think coaching is merely the ability to be aware of the mistakes people make and comment on them for the good of the client.

How many times have we had teachers, parents, bosses or anyone in a position of authority mouthing-off on their pet insight, thinking they are being helpful when they are simply being intrusive and irritating? They are also positioning themselves as being superior rather than relating to us as adult to adult'. Nowadays very few people accept being treated like children. Even children resent it. They also want to be treated like equals.

Coaching is a highly-skilled process of willing cooperation between a professional and a person who is ready and open to change, at the correct moment.

Otherwise all we're doing is akin to trying to teach a pig how to sing. What results is that we irritate the pig and waste our time – not a winning formula for making friends.

Coaching is not an easy exercise. It's intricate, sensitive and requires superior communication skills to make it work optimally. It is 'dynamic' meaning 'constantly changing' and the coach has to be extremely flexible and devoid of ego to focus solely on the clients' needs.

AHA Moments...

- Ask for Permission to coach in a Process of Willing Cooperation.

- Experience being coached by a skilled professional to understand the subtle nuances in coaching.

- Remember, coaching requires intricate, sensitive and superior communication skills to make it work optimally.

- Focus solely on the clients' need. Be flexible and devoid of ego.

Many candles can be kindled from one candle without diminishing it.

THE MIDRASH

6

Create a High Level of Trust Between Coach and Client

One prospective client who ran some nursing homes once said to me, "What do you know about running a nursing home?"

"Very little," I said. "But I do know how to ask the right questions; listen between the lines; be a good sounding board and assist my clients to achieve results beyond what they would normally do for themselves in a business setting."

For whatever reason, he was not convinced. Somehow he was cynical about either me or coaching or could not grasp the process. I, too, was not comfortable with him and could not see myself endlessly struggling to convince him that coaching was a good idea. So we parted, agreeing to disagree.

Coaching, once again, is intricate, delicate and requires enormous sensitivity to be valuable for both parties. It's vital that the trust level be beyond question for the process to work optimally and truthfully. It is a special relationship and certainly not for everyone.

On a few occasions I have walked away from profitable coaching contracts because I sensed that the trust level was not present.

In one situation I saw the CEO of a business use coaching technology as another tool to autocratically terrorize his staff with his new found insights. He did not quite grasp the value of what we were doing. He lacked awareness, had few people skills and was totally insensitive to his staff. I could see myself constantly having to explain basic human insights and reprimand him for being dictatorial with his people. He was not ready for this stretch and I was not prepared to teach basics to an overgrown, closed-minded child.

If coaches have to sell or strongly convince prospective clients to do business with them, the relationship will probably not work. Better to let it go than force the issue.

AHA Moments...

- Ensure the trust level is beyond question for the Coaching Process to work optimally and truthfully.

- Coaching is a special relationship – certainly not for everyone.

- If coaches have to sell or strongly convince prospective clients to do business with them, the relationship will probably not work. Better let it go than force the issue.

Wisdom begins in wonder.

SOCRATES

7

Set Clear Objectives based on the Client's Needs

Coaching is an event-driven process unlike consulting where the professionals come into a business, write plans and strategies, get paid and leave.

The coach agrees on specific, measurable targets to be achieved with the client and then walks in step with him/her until the goal has been achieved. Then they may set another target and continue to work together until that objective has been attained.

Paul W., a health-care professional for people who suffer from pain, was frustrated in his business because everything revolved around him. If he was not working with clients there was no money coming into the business. He found himself in conflict about his situation. Every month as he opened the doors to his business he felt he was starting fresh. There was no continuity and no ongoing contracts. When he completed a project he had to find a new one in order to survive. There was no residual income and he felt more and more vulnerable.

Many professionals or specialists in businesses feel the same as Paul.

I asked him, "What will give you continuous streams of income?"

He was creating a computerized program as a reference for clients so I said to him, "Is there a chance of you using the program for other health-care professionals, enabling them to increase their income by using your technology? If you can license the system and train them to your standards they could also create residual steams of income that would prop up their businesses?"

We talked about this possibility. He became very excited as the program was already almost complete, but he had never seen its value in this way. Now he could leverage the original investment, time and effort spent on preparing the program. He started to run seminars for allied, health-care professionals and is currently licensing the system as he had planned.

Paul had converted possibility to reality then to certainty and it has since led to other business opportunities.

AHA Moments...

- Unlike consulting where the professionals come into a business, write plans and strategies, get paid and leave, coaching is an event-driven process.

- The coach agrees on specific, measurable targets to be achieved with the client and then walks in step with him/her until the goal has been achieved.

Creativity often consists of merely turning up what is already there. Did you know that right and left shoes were thought up only a little more than a century ago?

BERNICE FITZ-GIBBON

8

Use Profiles as Tools for Improving Communication

In 1985, I first became aware of Profiles, or as some people call them, 'Assessment Tools.' At first I was extremely cynical and critical of these instruments, probably because I did not understand them fully.

What worried me was the tendency of some licensed practitioners and their followers to box people in categories of thinking styles and label them without taking the trouble to get to know them better. In the early days, before these instruments became popular, they were sometimes flippantly used as games by trainers to define who was like us and who was not like us. They certainly gave confidence to the 'in-group' but the others came out of the exercise believing they were inadequate. No wonder there was initial skepticism of this profiling invention.

A woman called me and asked to do a profile on my business management team. I had no idea exactly what she had in mind, but decided to go through the exercise for the experience. She started by interviewing the four of us, Mabs, Jim, Alice and me, then completed our profile reports.

She said, "Terry, you're a very private thinker. You get an idea, mull it over, talk about it quietly, get it clear in your mind and when you are ready to implement the project, you reveal it to the team. The problem is the team does not contribute to the creativity you initiated and is only involved in the implementation phase of your plan. This is not exciting for them. A better idea would be to come up with an idea, discuss it initially with Mabs who is a good alternative thinker and then ask the team for additional ideas to get them all involved in the process right from the initial stages. This means that they consider it to be their project too, and are not just working on your plan.

"The next step is to ask Jim to head the execution phase as he is a 'get it done' kind of guy and good at implementation.

"The final step is to discuss the financial implications with your office manager, Alice, to ensure you have sufficient cash flow to make the idea viable. She is cautious and caring and will probably slow down the process, but she adds rationality to the exercise."

These AHA moments were amazingly helpful to me and our management team loved the additional involvement and trust that had been injected into our company.

Now intrigued by the profile process, I went on a five day training program and started to immerse myself in this technology in order to grasp it more thoroughly.

Since those early days, I have consistently used Profiles to measure 'Thinking Styles' with almost all of my clients. They help me gain an initial insight into how I need to adapt my communication style to their way of doing things so that we are in sync with one another. It also becomes a reference point for both of us, resulting in a clearer understanding of each other.

My clients not only find it a useful tool but are also appreciative of the valuable insight the profiles provide.

As a professional coach, I stress that these tools are used only as a starting point in a coaching relationship – not as an end in itself. Often trainers use these tools to create a whole training program around the profiles, but **the objective should be to create insights and smooth communication leading to more profitable results, not to be the total focus of the exercise.**

Lois T. has worked for her brother-in-law, Vic, for five years, the last three managing the Internet side of his art print business. She's become more and more frustrated as he insists on micro-managing her every move. She can barely breathe at the office and Bob won't even listen to her concerns and complaints. She's not getting paid enough to put up with his demands and long working hours. She's tired of making him rich while she struggles to make ends meet. That's why Lois decided it's time to strike out on her own and start to develop her own online based 'art' business. She has lots of industry contacts and has created good relationships with many artists all over the world. Most have said they'll follow her wherever she goes.

Lois, very conservative by nature, has never taken much risk in her life. Although things seem to be falling in place she can't stop the constant worrying about everything she can't directly control. Unfortunately, she hasn't had a good night's sleep for over a month. Help!!!

'She's tired of making her boss rich while she struggles to make ends meet'.

This is the essence of why owners of businesses, big and small, lose their most trusted employees. They fail to recognize a basic need that everyone has built into their psyche – the need to be in control of their own lives. They don't necessarily need to own their own business, just to have the 'feeling' that they have a share in something that gives them the freedom to be their own boss.

If Vic only understood this he could have a creative, independent employee working with him who would be far more productive than she is now. Unfortunately he will never understand how to let go of his autocratic management style born of insecurity and fear of losing control.

I asked Lois to complete a 'Thinking Style' profile and a 'Values Assessment.' We discussed her hesitance in starting a new business and the challenges involved. Owning a business is not for everyone. We need to understand what we are getting into – the pros and cons – the benefits and challenges. Most people, if they understood the underlying commitment in advance about what really happens in business, would never think of accepting this responsibility.

Lois and I talked for hours about what she really wanted for her life – what she dreamed of and what counted for her to feel she was doing something worthwhile.

She ultimately came to the conclusion that owning her own business was going to be too stressful, lonely and demanding, but if she found the right partner who could compensate for those challenges, she could be a valuable and profitable co-worker.

She is currently seeking the right partner with the right chemistry to start a new venture.

AHA Moments...

- As a professional coach, use profiles as a starting point in a coaching relationship – not as an end in itself.

- The objective of using profiles should be to create insights and smooth communication leading to more profitable results, not to be the total focus of the exercise.

Don't be afraid to give up the good for the great.

KENNY ROGERS

9

Focus on Strengths, Not Weaknesses

People often express honesty and truthfulness believing it is in the best interests of the listener. Parents, teachers, bosses and managers do it all the time and then wonder why they receive strange reactions like hostility, tears, rudeness, aggressiveness, arguments and lack of cooperation from their victims.

Some call this process, 'constructive criticism.' **I have seldom found criticism constructive.** Most times I am patently aware of my mistakes and have often already moved forward to correct them without having some well-meaning individual drag me back into the past to rehash the error I have already corrected.

My question to myself is always: "Who asked for your opinion?" Obviously I do not often express this declaration as we are supposed to 'take it on the chin' and thank the insightful verbalizer for their contribution to our personal development. However, when some insensitive critical person shares their critical insights about me or about something I am doing, I sometimes, with forethought, respond assertively, especially when I know what I am doing is right for me.

A far more constructive way of coaching people is to focus on their strengths and tell them what they are. This is not as easy as it sounds. Many professions train and condition their disciples to look for weaknesses in processes, systems and people, and then eliminate the errors.

Over the years, I have discovered that engineers, scientists, accountants, lawyers, computer specialist and various other technical people have a tendency to be more critical in relationships than people in other professions. This is their training, or natural style of thinking, and this is how they often deal with life and others.

Many of my clients have come from these professions and I have had opportunities to coach them to soften their approach and attain far better results without losing effectiveness or reducing quality. In fact like removing grit from moving parts in an engine, they have reduced friction and attained superior results with greater cooperation.

Any time we criticize, we are playing the role of 'parent' asserting our superiority and making others feel inferior, or at best 'look bad.' **Surely it makes sense to comment on people's strengths, reinforce those strengths and ensure they see themselves in a better light.** It's obvious that we have to be genuine, sincere and appropriate. **The biggest challenge is to develop increased awareness by thinking about what others are doing well and simply tell them without expecting any reward.**

Ken Blanchard in 'The One Minute Manager' says: "Catch people doing things right and tell them."

One of my clients, **Warren S.**, bright and highly-intelligent, had an unfortunate manner with people. He believed strongly in telling the truth and would do just that even when it was inappropriate to do so. Consequently he made many enemies by simply being too honest with everyone he met and they would just run for their lives. Even though he was a highly-competent employee you can imagine what a liability he had become to his company. In desperation his boss called me one day and asked for my help.

Warren and I talked for several hours and despite my explaining how tentative his position was with the company, he genuinely appreciated the straight talk we had about his situation. Soon after our initial discussion he left the company with the blessing of the manager and found himself on a fast track, moving upwards in his career.

For him, the initial coaching was a breakthrough as he learned how to become more amenable and bite his tongue more often. He was amazed at how much more he was achieving with cooperation than with criticism. He was adamant about not changing his personality in order to accommodate others, but did get the message that tuning into others' needs and being a bit more understanding would take him further than his prior tendency.

He soon started to receive job offers and found himself moving up in the business world because of his ability to build teams and get the job done.

Warren still calls me regularly to resolve management issues with people on his team and we have remained close friends.

He knows I believe in him and his ability to perform in business. He is much more confident and at ease with himself and just this week was told by his new boss that he is in line for a further promotion.

AHA Moments...

- Catch people doing things right and tell them.

- Comment on people's strengths, reinforce those strengths and ensure they see themselves in a better light.

10

Add Energy to the Client's Cause

When we fail, as we all do at times, the energy is sucked out of us. It becomes increasingly difficult to energize ourselves for the challenges that confront us.

The underlying base of all coaching is to add energy and urgency to the client's arsenal of weapons. This isn't always how we feel, but we have no choice. We need to be upbeat otherwise we too suck out the energy from our vulnerable clients.

Andrew L. had just opened a new store in New York and was highly disappointed with the initial response to his promotional campaign. The following day he had a meeting with his financial backers and was debating what to tell them. He was really down and miserable and obviously afraid they might pull the plug on his dream venture.

I could tell his energy level was low from his voice. There was a tone of desperation in every word. He wanted me to commiserate with him, but I wasn't about to cooperate in his self-destruction.

I said, "Andrew, what do you think happened to cause this lack of response?"

I sat back in my chair and let him tell me the sad tale of his latest misfortune. When he was finished, I asked, "So what do you have to do differently to fix it?"

This time he was a little bit more enthusiastic as he outlined and verbalized his future plan. He said, "I have to set up more personal events in the store. Call influential people I know and invite them. Get my sales people to ask for referrals from each customer that visits the store. Quickly revamp my website to make it more user-friendly and ask for support from my friends."

As he verbalized his vision he physically became more excited.

This excitement almost always occurs when people verbally create their future rather than when they talk about the static past.

I asked him, "What barriers might block you?"

He thought about it and came up with some solutions. We completed the session with him promising to remain confident he could succeed and to convey that message and excitement about this vision to his staff and financial backers.

He thanked me profusely for the assistance in helping him see a different, more-optimistic picture.

Andrew was renewed and promised to behave that way at all times in his business environment.

AHA Moments...

- Add energy and urgency to the client. This is the underlying base of all coaching.

- Challenge clients to verbally create their future rather than focus on the static past. Greater energy and excitement result from the exercise.

*What the caterpillar calls the end of the world,
the master calls a butterfly.*

Richard Bach

11

Instill Confidence in the Client to Reach New Heights

One of the greatest diseases almost all of us suffer from is our inability to see ourselves in a better light. Others do, but somehow we don't believe them. They praise us or even point out things we do well and we can't see it, or we just reject the idea as being plain wrong. We may want to believe it, but that little voice in our head says, "No way."

Professor Higgins in Bernard Shaw's Pygmalion believed that he could transform Eliza Doolittle from a common flower girl on the streets into nobility. He even took a bet with Colonel Pickering that he could pass her off as aristocracy within a short time.

All he had to do was teach her to speak the King's English, teach her etiquette and manners, dress her appropriately and she would pass the test. She did, but at the end of the story she married Freddy, not Professor Higgins. She said, "He still saw me as a flower girl. Freddy sees me as I am today."

If there is any secret in successful coaching, this is it.

The coach sees the client as they could be, not as they are today, and communicates that belief to the client again and again until it becomes a reality.

Melissa R. worked in a not-for-profit business charged with raising money for a number of projects. She felt she was being underutilized and this was borne out by the amount of money she was earning. She was struggling to make ends meet and could not see herself surviving in the organization. She was fully aware that she could earn more if she was more productive, as her income was based on performance. However, she was limited by her thinking and by not having sufficient confidence to produce more business.

We talked about the lack of money which had paralyzed her and I said, "I know you can do more business. In fact, I think you can produce 300% more than you are doing right now in the next six months."

She started to laugh and said, "You're crazy. I could never do that!"

I asked, "If you could do that amount what difference would it make to your personal financial situation?"

She replied with a touch of cynical enthusiasm, "It would make a huge difference and I would not have this anxiety I feel now."

So I said, "Let's break the big number down to a monthly amount." We did that, and then to a weekly amount.

I asked, "How do you feel about this weekly figure? Is that possible for you?"

She said, "Maybe," this time with a little more excitement.

We explored some new ideas and came to the conclusion that if she focused on a few larger clients who were already receptive to her, she could do it.

We examined other activities that absorbed her time with little return and she agreed to cut down on those activities and start looking at areas where she could be more productive.

Then she started to become really excited.

Six months later she wrote this note:

"I am now making more money than I ever thought possible. I have met the goal which you encouraged me to set (and frankly I didn't think it was possible). I now have the confidence that I can increase revenues by 300% for the following year! And substantially increase my own bank account!"

AHA Moments...

- See clients as they could be, not as they are today.

- Communicate their potential to them again and again until it becomes a reality.

12

Access Our Intuition – Document the Vision – Create the Plan

Many business analysts or consultants tell business owners to start their companies by first creating a plan. The reality is that writing the plan is the second or third part of the process, not the first.

We start any new project or venture with a vision. We do this by accessing our intuition. Sometimes it is clear – sometimes not. First, we need to envision the picture of what it looks like, not now, but say in 12 months from now, or two years or even more into the future. The more concrete the picture, the easier it becomes to capture. Of course this is all initially in our head and we may have to share it with others affected, to gain their support and commitment.

Sometimes only owners of businesses have the vision. That's why it's vital they share it with everyone and gain buy-in, making sure everyone on the team feels part of the family. If other members of the team don't get it and have reservations about the vision, they're likely to devastate the energy of the group and need to go, sooner rather than later. This is a tough step in any relationship and ultimately is the making of the leader. Leaders have to be clear about their direction and after negotiations with partners and colleagues need to take a stand on the path they have chosen. If not, the vision becomes cloudy as everyone's input stalls the action required and nothing happens.

Documenting the vision clearly is the next step. Just talking about it is a good start, but it becomes contaminated if not set on paper.

Accessing our intuition is not just an airy-fairy act, but an initial, vital piece of the puzzle in creating a concrete plan for a business.

Many business owners find this process difficult. That's why using an outside catalyst, like a business coach, can be extremely helpful in setting up the process for the company and following it through to fruition.

Kevin B. owns a construction company and grew-up in the industry. Unfortunately, like most business owners, he was not trained in management and always felt more comfortable on the building sites supervising others to achieve the targets set. He was driven by the daily crises that cropped up constantly and therefore became the natural solver of all these issues. This meant that everyone stopped making decisions because Kevin was the guy everyone referred to if decisions were to be made – even if he wasn't present at the time. In fact, Kevin became *Superman* and everyone just stood around and watched *Superman* work until virtually nothing was being done without Kevin signing off on it.

When we first met, Kevin told me how busy he was and then

proceeded to miss a couple of appointments. He also didn't follow up on emails.

It was true! He was so busy he could not possibly handle all the tasks on his plate. Even *Superman* couldn't do it.

I laughed when I realized what had been going on because I too had been *Superman* at one time in my business and had become so good at what I was doing that secretly, and sometimes not so secretly, my staff called me The Ayatollah. I was so good that everyone around me stopped growing because they realized, or so they thought, they would never be as good as *Superman*.

It was only when a colleague visited my operation and dramatically and bluntly told me that my business and family was going to go down the tubes if I didn't delegate some responsible results to my people. Only then did I start to change. I wrote a plan for the business outlining what results were to be achieved by whom and by what date. Not only was it a turning point in my life, but also the start of a *Quantum Leap* in my business as I began to focus on what counted for me.

I shared this experience with Kevin and we started the same process. He very quickly grasped the concept and revamped his business, apportioning greater responsibility to his team. He's now on a completely different track and his business will continue to improve dramatically as he continues to fully utilize his talented team.

What is important to note is that Kevin is implementing the change. He wrote the Plan and he decided where to invest his time for best results. I just act as a coach, asking 'what if' type questions and he fills in the blanks and makes it happen. I am not his guru. I am not a consultant. We are just two adults working like adults together to accomplish a planned, desired

result in a systematic manner as opposed to the hodge-podge style he previously used.

AHA Moments...

- Coach clients to access their intuition. This is not just an airy-fairy act, but an initial, vital piece of the puzzle in creating a concrete plan for a business.

- Encourage clients to visualize a concrete vision of the future for their businesses.

- Challenge clients to use clear word-pictures – not just conceptual language.

- Remember: The reality is that writing the plan is the second or third part of the process not the first.

13

Eliminate Doubt and Feelings of Inadequacy

Married for more than 40 years, the **Websters** have always wanted to have their own business. It's been their dream! Now retired, they have the time and money to start their own business and want to do something out of their home.

They have a shared passion for exotic plants and have even engineered several unique orchids that might be ideal to market online. They've got lots of ideas but can't seem to get started. Perhaps it's because they've procrastinated for years and years.

Passion in any business is the best starting point for being successful, but it is only a starting point. Carl and Karen Webster have never been in business before and although they have many friends who have been successful in running their own businesses, they don't have any inkling as to what's involved. Little do they know how many businesses fail and simply fade away into dust.

Of course they have skills and talents in their chosen field, combined with endless patience and enthusiasm, but what they lack is a full understanding of the mechanics and challenges.

This was what I initially discussed with them during our first coaching session. They asked questions and I threw questions back at them to show the answers they want are actually within them. I suggested they read some books on starting a home business. We then dialogued on what they saw as their ideal business scenario. They wrote a draft of what they felt was vital and important, in the present tense in short sentences and we talked about the new picture they could now clearly envision.

We discussed marketing online and how to prepare themselves for this challenge. I gave them some leads to talk to experts in that field and slowly the momentum began to grow as their belief in this late-blooming project began to take shape. Mostly I have just had to bolster their confidence – to give them the feeling that they are not alone and simply be around when they need to talk.

Virtually all business owners feel lonely at times and support is one of the major benefits we can supply.

In a year or so the Webster's will laugh at their hesitance about starting the business, but right now it is real and very frightening for them as they contemplate the risks and possible disasters. However, they are intelligent people who are open-minded to change and want to do more with their lives even if they sometimes feel they may have missed the boat. They will be fine and will make it work. I believe in them.

All business owners face moments of doubt, feelings of inadequacy, and/or fear of failure.

Most people have toyed with the idea of starting their own businesses, but only those who have taken the plunge know what it is to wake-up very early in the mornings half-dreaming of things going wrong in the business. These are subconscious fears flooding our minds when we are at our most vulnerable – half-asleep, in bed, waiting for the day to begin. Sometimes when we are off-guard, in the car, walking or waiting for our next appointment, the same thing happens.

How do we shut-down that little green man on our shoulder who constantly reminds us by whispering in our ear?

"You're going down the tubes!"

I needed to change the inner conversation to something much more positive, and after playing around with a few affirmations finally came up with a simple Mantra that works for my clients.

"I have the Power. I make the Decisions."

Test it out by quietly saying it to yourself a few times during the day – early in the morning, before going to sleep and especially before any challenging moments.

See if it works for you, but test it for at least 14 days.

Let me know what happens?

AHA Moments…

- Recognize that all business owners face moments of doubt, feelings of inadequacy and/or fear of failure.

- Help clients to eliminate doubt by coaching them with intuitive questions.

- Remind clients that they have the Power. They make the Decisions.

14

Show Genuine Belief in the Client's Ability to Change

George T. is a bright young professional. He could have been a dentist if he wanted to, but instead decided to run a hands-on business. He is very intense and no one could accuse him of being casual. He discovered that this driving focus was interfering with his ability to create and maintain relationships at home, socially and in business. His approach to everything was either black or white – no gray areas existed in his world.

He told me that he had a wonderful relationship with his mother and confided in her regularly. This was his safety valve.

Recently his wife said to him, "Your Mom seems to be upset with me. Did I do something to upset her that you know of?"

He shrugged it off without an answer, but told me that his Mom, being very loyal to him, probably felt negative towards his wife because of the things he had mentioned about her over the previous months.

Now he was in a pickle. He could not tell his wife what he had done and he had obviously prejudiced his Mom towards her. I asked him:

"What do you think you can do to improve your Mom's attitude towards your wife?"

He said, "I suppose I should talk to her and explain that things in my relationship with my wife have improved dramatically since we last talked. Maybe her attitude would change."

I agreed, "That sounds like a good strategy. Try it."

He seemed relieved, but most important was his response to this dialogue.

He said, "I didn't realize how careful I have to be with comments I make to others, especially to close family members. I need to raise my level of awareness."

This was a breakthrough AHA for him because up to now he had been far too liberal in expressing possible hurtful remarks.

For a moment I asked if I could change hats from being coach to mentor. He agreed. So I explained that in South Africa where I come from, there is an African saying: 'The person who delivers the message first is believed.'

In business politics, the person who tells the boss their version of a story first, has more chance of being believed than the person who relates it later.

This means that if there is some piece of information that could be controversial, tell the boss immediately – the sooner the better. Bosses in business hate nasty surprises. They do not like to be vulnerable or look stupid because things have gone wrong somewhere in their area of control and others discovered it before they did.

Also, behavior in one situation is often an indicator that this is a pattern reproducing itself in other situations.

A new client, **Cynthia**, approached me to help solve the problems she was having at work. All she heard from her boss was: "You're not fitting in here! You need to change!" The big problem for Cynthia was she had no idea how to go about it and wasn't even certain what her boss disapproved of.

The light came on for Cynthia once we started the coaching. She clearly saw how easy it was for her to create a new future, day-by-day, in easy-to-do, small steps. After all, coaching is event-driven and the whole process revolves around taking small steps to change the way we normally do things. As long as we clearly picture the steps we need to take in the right context and feel motivated to move in that direction the process is easy to accomplish.

Cynthia's *experience with coaching is best described in a letter she sent to me.*

I used to argue all the time. I could exhaust anybody by arguing. I would not even fully listen to them, just cut them off and give my point of view. For some reason it was so important for me to be heard and for my opinion to be put out there. When people were wrong I always had to tell them that they were wrong. My most used word was 'no'. I never took time to understand what people meant – just that they heard what I wanted to say. I did not know how to listen and everyone complained about me. I even lost my clients despite my having initiated the largest deals in the portfolio. Everyone and I mean everyone, spoke about my enthusiasm and energy, but followed it up with the fact that I didn't listen. I tried to pretend to listen, but people are not as stupid as I thought they were. They knew. No one knew how to teach me to listen until I received coaching. Not to mention that I felt that I was the only one with this problem.

My manager recommended coaching for me and I'm sure he had no idea what the effect would be. He had no idea that it would be the single best thing ever to happen to me, not only as a professional, but also as a woman. I'm sure he believed I would finally see what I was doing wrong and hopefully stop doing that, or at least just see what I was doing badly. But I do not think he expected that I would grow so much as a person and certainly not make such huge progress. He gave me loads of feedback about my behavior, and how I kept pissing off people, and how I was creating personal destructive relationships, but I never really understood him, so I just kept on doing what I thought he meant, and I kept on alienating everybody around me.

He was not telling me what I should be doing, but what I was doing wrong, so it wasn't positive feedback, just destructive criticism which he thought was hugely constructive.

During my first coaching session, I cried when my coach explained to me how to do it. The key lay in my insecurity, and in that I felt I always needed to participate by talking. I would take every opportunity to make sure everything was about me. I was unintentionally taking away from everyone, the opportunity of being heard. Also, I would jump to conclusions instead of asking questions to get a better understanding of what they meant or were trying to say. I would just interrupt the conversation with "no" and fill in my part. I would not give people a chance to explain themselves.

Finally, I got the 'AHA' of what I was doing to piss-off everyone. I felt so free, I cried. I wanted so badly to stop hurting people and turning them away from me in my work and all I was getting was criticism on how badly I was doing with people. Finally my coach broke it down for me into small steps and I was free. I discovered that I was acting from insecurity, and from wanting to be heard, fearing that I would be left out. I felt I needed to go and find the light. The light, I thought, was inside me and if I just talked to impress and had the light shine on me and what I wanted, I thought I was fine.

Every time I opened my mouth I fell into someone else's impression of me. And the worse it got the more I talked and the more I talked the worse it got. My coach told me to just shut up and focus on the other person. And I did, and it worked. I discovered from coaching that the more I talk the more people judge me. Before that I always thought the more I talked the more interesting I seemed to be, or people thought I was. I thought talking meant that they would see me as a thinker, but I realized that all that people were doing was using my words to hurt and judge me.

So, I started listening more to them. This gave me the power to decide when people could judge me, or on what I allowed them to judge me.

I started asking myself, "Do I really need to say something? Can I add something to this conversation?"

I just shut up, and allowed people to talk.

I started to give people the experience of genuinely being listened to.

I figured out during my coaching sessions that since I liked being listened to so much, other people also had the same feeling. So I helped them have that experience and they didn't judge me so much. I stopped feeling that I had to impress them by talking so much.

Change is never easy!

Now that Cynthia had the key, she started to engage people in conversations and dialogue instead of talking at them. She decided to test out her newly found insight with her supervisor. She asked genuine questions about him and his family. Amazingly, their uneasy relationship started to thaw and became a little less formal as they found out more about each other.

One day after they had jointly visited a client, he invited her home to meet his family. She met his wife and played with his three kids for a while that evening and felt as though she was part of their family, albeit only for a few hours. She went home that night feeling elated at this unexpected sense of belonging and immediately felt she could now relate more closely to her supervisor. From that day on there was a completely different caliber of working relationship.

I coached Cynthia to write a Function Results Description with the major goal of assisting her Supervisor to attain his targets for the year. Of course this perspective made a huge difference to his impression of her. He realized that she was there to ensure that he reached his targets rather than her being the needy, high profile, high maintenance associate that she had been previously.

She started to take on more responsibility to achieve the agreed results and as a unified team the two combined smoothly and seamlessly with one another. The business started to come in quickly and the trust level in this small team inspired them to take on more initiatives. Cynthia started to call-on additional clients and committed herself to bring in extra business. Her supervisor experienced her unconditional support. All the original friction that had hindered their progress previously, disappeared and was replaced with two respectful adults synergizing their efforts to not only achieve their joint, targeted goals, but go beyond what they had ever imagined was possible.

Came the final appraisal of the year and they both achieved the highest possible grades for performance, far exceeding their original set targets.

For Cynthia, who was on the brink of being fired for being disruptive and ineffective, this was a reward beyond what she or anyone else believed was possible in just eight months.

Her boss was genuinely pleased with the remarkable transition, but there was always the odd remark about the 'Old Cynthia'. Each time he said that, he eroded her fragile confidence by pulling her back into the past.

I explained to her that changing is never easy because people around us do not like us to change. It seems to upset their equilibrium. I suggested she go to all the people who cared about her, tell them she was working on changing her behavior and ask for their support. She did just that and found that the strategy made her transition much easier. Most of her friends and colleagues were supportive and gave her positive feedback.

Unfortunately most education and a great deal of training is driven by telling others what to do based on our knowledge and our agendas, rather than coaching our employees to find their own personal method to implement new ways of doing things within their own context, not the coach's context.

Be there as a friend, confidant, advisor and supporter.

AHA Moments...

- Show genuine belief in our client's ability to change.

- Remind clients that change is never easy because people around us do not like us to change. It seems to upset their equilibrium.

- Coach our employees to find their own personal method to implement new ways of doing things within their own context, not the coach's context.

- Always be there as a friend, confidant, advisor and supporter

Ideas won't keep: something must be done about them.

ALFRED NORTH WHITEHEAD

PART III
The Elements of Business Coaching

15

Start with a Vision not Goals

There is much talk today about setting goals. Most people agree it's a good idea, but few people set them and fewer follow through to achieve the original target they set for themselves. What happens is they fail and feel so guilty about failing that they stop committing themselves because the fear of failure is so painful.

The solution is to start with a vision – not goals. It's a simple process, but not that easy to implement.

We ask ourselves:

- What do I see for myself over the next year?

- What result would be most pleasing?

- What does my business look like in twelve months from now at its very best, without limitations of effort, money or time?

Now write the answers down on a sheet of paper or on a computer.

Each sentence should be:

- Short (no more than one or two lines)

- Written in the present tense

- Perceived, as though it had already been achieved.

As described in Part II of this book, this is called 'Accessing our Intuition.' It's a process of imagination that should be documented lest it simply disappears as our minds are overtaken by millions of other stimuli that demand our attention.

Once we have a clear vision that evokes our passion we're ready to start writing goals that reflect our deepest desires.

Maureen P. is a single mother of two teenagers, Cindy, 16, and Brian, 18. Now that both kids are driving and preoccupied outside the home Maureen has the time and desire to do something more with her life. She's decided to start her own home-based business. For years Maureen's been making hand-made soaps for her family and friends. Now she wants to turn it into a business. However, she's overwhelmed with all the things she needs to do and is having trouble getting started.

Step one was to have Maureen verbalize what she wanted to do by creating a clear vision of the 'Ideal Situation'.

I asked, "Tell me what you see in the future for your business? Describe it in short sentences in the present tense as though you have already achieved it. There are no limitations of energy, time or money."

As she started to tell me I asked her to write down the list and email it to me. Once she had completed the task she said she felt so much clearer about what she wanted for her business.

I then asked her to look at her list and visualize what she saw happening after 12 months, six months and after the first three months.

I then asked, "What is really happening at present?"

She started to tell me and then wrote down exactly what was happening now. Once she had verbalized and then documented the situations she was able to clearly see what she had to do to move from 'reality' to the 'ideal' scenario.

Now she had documented a broad time schedule for her first year of running her business and the feeling of being overwhelmed suddenly dissipated as the picture of what she had to do became clearer, easier to anticipate and manageable.

This is 'Accessing our Intuition,' as discussed in Chapter 12. As part of the process I challenge all my clients to document what they have told me. It is amazing to hear the sudden release of tension in their voices as they explain the new future they have just created.

Nothing in coaching is more satisfying than hearing clients who were previously overwhelmed, stuck and dispirited suddenly realize the limitations they had so carefully constructed for themselves have been easily washed away by a simple process and replaced by such an exciting possibility.

Although it looks and sounds easy to do, a highly-trained coach is vital to take the process through to a successful conclusion.

Maureen is now on her way to making her dream come true and, more importantly, knows in her heart that it will work and she can create a highly-profitable business that will secure her future.

AHA Moments...

- Start with vision. Not goals. It's a simple process, but not always easy to implement.

- Coach clients to develop a clear vision that evokes their passion then to write goals that reflect their deepest desires.

16

Listen Actively – Not Passively

Seldom in our lives do we have the experience of 'being genuinely listened to.' Most of us are far too busy to be bothered by others and their concerns because we are focused on our own issues and how to resolve them.

Even within families we may have had the experience of wanting to talk openly about an issue, but somehow never felt that the moment was right to talk about it. Or maybe the moment was right, we started to talk and suddenly felt the supposed listener was not listening at all and may even have shown irritation at being hijacked as a victim of the exercise.

Dr. Thomas Gordon in his book, *Parent Effectiveness Training*, talks about the way psychologists are trained to listen and how those skills could be useful in almost all everyday contacts with people around us. He calls the process 'Active Listening' which looks more like 'Active Questioning' than listening. The idea is to listen to the underlying issues beneath the words or between the lines rather than the content that is being verbalized. Secondly, listen non-judgmentally without prejudice.

In his weekly coaching call, **Steve G.** asked me, "Have you ever had a boss talk to one of your staff members and give them instructions without informing you – their manager?"

I answered, "So your boss by-passed you, gave instructions to one of your people and left you out of the loop? That must have irritated you!"

"I was fuming!" he said. "One of my people came and asked me whether he was their new boss instead of me."

"That must have made you feel even worse."

"Yes! I felt that he had completely undermined my authority and made me look stupid in the eyes of my group."

"So you are going to talk to him about it?" I asked.

"Yes. I'll bring it up in our weekly meeting on Thursday and tell him that his behavior was unacceptable."

Once I had created an opportunity for Steve to express what was really bothering him, he felt much better. Talking about it, without feeling I was judging him, made it easier for him to tell me his story.

The real issue was not that his boss gave instructions to his group without informing him, it was that he felt his boss 'undermined his authority which made him feel stupid and undervalued.'

Active Listening is accessing what is happening underneath the words not necessarily what is initially being said on the surface.

AHA Moments...

- Give clients the experience of "being genuinely listened to."

- Active Listening is accessing what is happening underneath the words not necessarily what is initially being said on the surface.

Practice is the best of all instructors.

Publilius Syrus

17

Practice Correctly

We have all heard the old adage, 'Practice makes perfect.' This is probably true. More relevant, however, is that 'practice makes permanent' said Gary Wiren from the PGA. If we were practicing a golf shot or a tennis shot or a presentation and were trying to master it, we would have to be sure what we were practicing was the right shot not the wrong one.

Often small business owners want to develop skills in their business to increase their effectiveness. They may pick up some ideas from others or even from books, but find that the new method doesn't give them the result they were hoping to attain.

This is why an experienced professional coach is so important. The small business owner could so easily think what they're trying to implement is the right way, when actually making the wrong thing more permanently a part of their repertoire.

One of the reasons why this area of practice is so important is that we focus on another old adage. 'We learn from our mistakes.' Also probably true, but if we see ourselves as failing and try to correct that pattern, we are still reinforcing the 'wrong way' by focusing on it. We may even see ourselves as failing and try to dig ourselves out of the hole. Our mental attitude is then negative. Correcting this take lots of effort and is sometimes very painful.

When we hear people say, "I will try to..." it indicates immediately that they are expecting to fail, but will put on a jolly good show to impress us so that when they do what they expect, which is to fail, they have a great alibi. Somehow they were brought up to believe that a great alibi is a replacement for a good performance.

A better way is to determine what we are doing 'right,' focus on it and do it more often. Then our mental attitude is automatically more positive because we see ourselves as being successful and even more effective.

There is no doubt that when we are in a good frame of mind, we have more energy and can perform more successfully.

By now you will have guessed that I play golf. For me playing golf is a great way to gauge how people around me conduct their lives – either personally or in business. What we do on the golf course is exactly how we run our lives off the course.

Nothing surprises me more than when there are water hazards and I hear my partners say things like: "I hate hitting over water! I always mess up! I can't seem to get it right!" Then they hit the ball into the water and say: "You see! I told you. I can't do that! I always go in the water!"

Then the next time they hope to have a different result with the same undermining mindset they utilized previously. There's something wrong here!

The point is we can't expect a positive result if our thinking, our attitude and mindset are the same as they were when we originally failed. We have to create a whole new style of thinking, attitude and mindset to create a different result. The same truth exists in all aspects of our lives.

If we are failing in business and want to succeed we need to make some major adjustments. One of them is to find out what we are doing right and do it more often. Eliminate the things we are doing wrong and recognize – 'we learn from our mistakes, but we grow from our successes.'

AHA Moments...

- Take note that 'practice makes perfect' is probably true, but more relevant is – "practice makes permanent."

- 'Just do it' the Nike Ad says. When we say: "I will try to…" it indicates we are expecting to fail and are simply creating an alibi to justify it.

- Find out what we are doing right and do it more often.

- Remember – 'We learn from our mistakes, but we grow from our successes.'

What we see depends mainly on what we look for.

JOHN LUBBOCK

18

Be Clear!

Thomas K., an American friend of mine from New York, now living in London, once remarked, "I love England. This is such a civilized culture." He went on to explain: "English culture is so polite, gentle and non-intrusive compared with the direct communication I am used to in New York."

Working in London as I did over a number of years, I recognized what he was saying, comparing this experience with being in The Netherlands or even in South Africa where I was born and started my career. What I also noticed was that my language was much more direct than that of many people in the UK.

If something was not clear, I would always ask for clarification by saying: "How do you mean?" or "Can you explain that again? It's not clear for me."

Once in The Netherlands, I was doing business with a client company and the receptionist said to me, "Do you know that you are very rude on the telephone?"

I was horrified as I always thought I was extremely professional on the telephone.

So I asked, "How do you mean?"

She answered, "You never start the call by announcing your name. You just ask for the person you want to speak to and that is very rude in The Netherlands. You think we are not important enough to identify yourself first, before asking to speak to our boss."

Talk about Cultural Differences!!

I felt as if I had just crawled out of cheese, but the receptionist was right and clear.

Never again did I make that mistake, and even now in the USA I always answer the phone by announcing my name and when phoning out, do the same.

My point is that this 'dressing down' was extremely direct and would never happen in England. The locals would just accept my lack of class, but never comment on it.

How would I ever know how out of place I was without someone telling me?

Therefore, I always pepper my conversation or talks with questions like: "Is this clear?"

It's important to ensure our communication is understood as intended and if things are not clear for me, I always ask for clarification.

In business it is vital that we are not just understood, but that we are not misunderstood. The cost of correcting mistakes, in time and money, can be a huge drain on company resources.

AHA Moments...

- Let's make sure that we are not just understood, but that we're not misunderstood.

- Remember that the high cost of correcting mistakes, in time and money, is a huge drain on a business.

Human diversity makes tolerance more than a virtue; it makes it a requirement for survival.

RENE DUBOS

19

Challenge Clients

A coach can challenge clients to achieve goals far beyond anything they have ever conceived of previously as being a possibility.

This allows the client to imagine something that is brand new with no preconceived ideas about what it would look like. This creates greater flexibility for thinking that is often severely limited by previous painful failures that blocked us in the past. Often unable to move into the future without imagining a disaster about to happen, we too often settle for a small jump that is safe until we are ready to venture forward again outside of our comfort zone.

This incremental improvement can be increased exponentially when we raise our performance beyond what we would normally expect for ourselves.

Kathy P. was waiting for her boss to give her a target for the following year and during our discussion I suggested she set her own goals for the coming twelve months. At first she was reluctant to take this initiative because it was customary for her boss to provide her with his expectations for the year.

I asked, "What do you have to lose by writing a plan for the year based on your highest expectations?"

She thought for a moment, hesitated as she battled with herself and then said defiantly, "Why not?"

Suddenly she looked different. A confident smile creased her face as she realized that she was free to make her own decisions about the coming year and how it would look. She also understood she now would be working on her vision, aligned with that of her boss, but it was her vision, not his. That was very attractive.

She crafted the plan over a few days, with obvious delight, as though she was now her own boss with no restrictions. She now had a totally different mind-set towards her career as she realized what she was capable of achieving. All of a sudden she had arrived and she liked it.

When she had fine-tuned the document, she presented it to her boss and asked if it met his criteria for fulfilling his expectations for the coming year.

He was delighted that she had taken the initiative and was especially excited about the high standards she had set for herself – some higher than what he would have expected from her. It was as if he had discovered a jewel in the business, without knowing she was always there ready to serve – a blossom waiting to bloom.

What had the coach done? Not much, except he saw Kathy as she could be rather than as she was. He told her what he saw, and she too got the picture of the new Kathy.

She knew she would never be the same again.

AHA Moments…

- Ask our clients to write a plan based on their highest expectations.

- Challenge clients to achieve a goal far beyond anything they ever conceived of previously as being a possibility.

Don't compromise yourself; you're all you've got.

JANICE JOPLIN

20

Clarify Commitment

When I started my first company, one of my mentors, Dick Morgal, discussed the word 'commitment' with me. Although I was relatively new to business that word became a vital element in my understanding of human values. He had noticed some of the people who worked with me were a bit casual about sticking to their word or following through on their promises. I too was casual about things like being on time. So we talked about this characteristic in people's behavior.

He explained, "Being on time means 15 minutes early for an appointment."

I argued with him initially, but soon understood what he meant. I thought being so early was extreme. Then one of my international colleagues, Duncan Ehlers, reinforced this idea by saying: **"When we are early we control the situation. When we are late or just on time, the situation controls us."**

This does not mean we need to be control freaks. It just means we give ourselves a chance of being able to present ourselves at our very best rather than worrying about the uncertainties that crop up when we are in a frenzied rush. Personally, this was a huge challenge for me because I often like to push the envelope by challenging myself to be just in time to fit in one last task before moving on to the next obligation. These two wise men impressed on me that being late for appointments is disrespectful and shows the other party we don't care much for them. It's arrogant.

I didn't want to be disrespectful or arrogant. Initially I just didn't understand the effect that it had on others so I cleaned up my act immediately.

Another insight struck me. Not following through on my word could cause anxiety in others because lack of consistency evokes a sense of distrust which could erode their belief in me.

No way can we be credible in any relationships without people trusting us, so we are not talking about a choice. This is an absolute certainly in the English speaking world, because this is one of the ways we value professionalism.

AHA Moments…

- Test this idea – "When we are early we control the situation. When we are late or just on time, the situation controls us."

- Never forget – "Our credibility in any relationship is built on trust."

*We don't quit playing because we get old.
We get old because we quit playing.*

OLIVER WENDELL HOLMES

21

Adapt to Cultural Differences

When I lived in Europe I soon discovered that being on time is not nearly as important to some cultures as it is in ours.

Edward T. Hall in his book, *Time - the Dance of Life* makes a distinction between 'monochronic' and 'polychronic' cultures.

He says: English, Scandinavian, German, and Dutch speaking people of the world are distinctly monochronic – meaning, time is the defining value of their culture.

Polychronic people such as French, Italian, Portuguese and Spanish speaking people, as well as people from Africa and the Middle East, place more emphasis on relationships than on time, as the defining value of their culture.

Soon after coming to the USA in 1998, we were visited by friends from Mexico. We were invited to a dinner function at 7 PM. My wife and I called for them at their hotel at 6:45 PM, but they were not ready to go and we finally left for the party at 7:30 PM. Our friend and his wife were not the least concerned about being late.

My wife and I were a bit concerned, but did not let it bother us. En route to the party I explained the distinction to them about monochronic and polychronic and he laughed uproariously about this new insight.

Monochronic People	Polychronic People
Do one thing at a time	Do many things at once
Concentrate on the job	Highly distracted and subject to interruptions
Low-context and need information	High-context and already have information
Committed to the job	Committed to people
Adhere religiously to plans	Change plans often and easily
Concerned about not disturbing others. Follows rules of privacy and consideration	More concerned with relations (family, friends, close business associates) than with privacy.
Shows great respect for private property, seldom borrow or lend	Borrow and lend things often and easily
Emphasizes promptness	Base promptness on the relationship
Accustomed to short-term relationships	Strong tendency to build lifetime relationships

Source: Hall and Hall

When we finally arrived at our destination, the hostess was seriously worried about us and had delayed serving the food until we had arrived. We had definitely inconvenienced our hosts and their guests, but they were gracious and never said a word about it.

Our Mexican guest was horrified when the party ended at 9:30 PM and we were the last ones to leave. He had obviously expected the celebration to last well into the wee hours of the morning with dancing and drinking and was disappointed. However, our earlier discussion had a made a huge impression on him and he just laughed again at the innocuous way we 'Monos' as he put it, celebrate. I am sure that he felt highly secure about being a 'Poly' rather than a 'Mono.'

To go back to commitment, whether we are monochronic or polychronic we need to be committed to being consistent in our relationships in order to eliminate the friction that erodes the vital connection necessary in business.

Dr. Peter Robertson, a management consultant and colleague I once worked with in The Netherlands, told me that the major distinction he observed in effective top-level management was that they knew themselves well. The result was consistency in their behavior. He went on to say, "Inconsistency in behavior breeds anxiety in others" – a good insight for owners and managers of businesses.

Once while working in Belgium with a management team from a business in Ghent, the group told me why they were different from their Dutch neighbors.

They said if they made a mistake the Dutchman would immediately tell them what they had done wrong. The Belgian in the group would, however, politely ask questions about the mistake and allow the perpetrator to discover the error themselves. The Englishman would notice the mistake, never say a word, but believe the perpetrator was an idiot.

AHA Moments…

- English, Scandinavian, German, and Dutch speaking people of the world are distinctly monochronic — meaning time is the defining value of their culture.

- Polychronic people such as French, Italian, Spanish and Portuguese speaking people, as well as people from Africa and The Middle East place more emphasis on relationships than on time as the defining value of their culture.

- Regardless of differences in culture, we need to be highly sensitive to the diverse ways people from other places process information and therefore respond.

- Ensure we never assume people from other areas, regions, or countries are the same as us.

22

Talk 'I Language' not 'You Language'

Dr Thomas Gordon in his book *Parent Effectiveness Training* cites an example of a teenager coming home late one night and the distraught parents yell: "Where have you been? What have you been doing? Do you have no consideration for us? We agreed you would be home much earlier than this!"

The young person was sucked into making excuses and alibis for her misdemeanor to protect herself.

Dr Gordon calls this, 'You Language' meaning the parents are pouring out their anger on the hapless teenager by constantly emphasizing 'You' in their speech.

He goes onto say that, 'Anger' is always a secondary emotion. In this instance the parents could have communicated what they were experiencing just before the child returned home and said what was genuinely on their minds.

'I language' – that is: "I was so worried about you. Are you OK? Did something go wrong? Come here and give me a hug…"

This is what they were genuinely feeling, but somehow we often fail to express these primary emotions and revert instead to using power. This means we communicate like 'Parents' talking to a naughty 'Child.'

Once again, neither children, teenagers or adults like to be 'talked at.' We want to speak and be spoken to as adults talking to adults. This means the speaker respects us as responsible grownups and does not immediately assume we are wrong and irresponsible.

This also means we do not give solutions to problems. We allow the listeners to come up with their own solutions. We learn to shrug our shoulders more often when asked: "How do I …" type questions and allow them to resolve their own issues. This is how we become responsible adults and they become adults too, accountable for their own results.

If we want to have people in our companies behave like adults, take responsibility and resolve their own issues, we may need to adjust our style of communication from 'Parent to Child' or 'You' language to 'Adult to Adult' or 'I' language.

This is easy to say, but can be hard to do without practice and some coaching.

AHA Moments…

- Neither children, teenagers or adults like to be 'talked at.' Let's speak and be spoken to as adults talking to adults.

- Let's stop giving solutions to problems – rather allow others to come up with their own solutions.

People who get on in this world are people who get up and look for the circumstances they want and if they can't find them, make them.

GEORGE BERNARD SHAW

23

Believe in Our Ability to Make a Difference

As a coach, every contact I make with people reminds me to see my clients as they could be at their very best, rather than as they are now. This does not mean they are not at their very best now, but if they are open to growth and development, they are by definition open to change.

I am committed to making a difference in people's lives if they are open to change.

Every coaching session is an opportunity to make a difference in my clients' lives. What I mean is that I look for something in our dialogue that will spark a new insight in the life of the client.

The definition of insight is:

in·sight (ĭn'sīt') *n* – "The capacity to discern the true nature of a situation."

It is the possibility to create an "AHA" moment.

a·ha (ä-hä') *interj.* Used to express surprise, pleasure, or triumph.

Charles M. and I talked about the challenges he faced in his printing company.

He was trying to determine what was preventing him from generating additional revenue to improve cash flow. Like most business people in this type of pressure situation, he immediately jumped into the area of 'possible solutions' rather than first defining the 'problem.'

He admitted that he was uncomfortable running this kind of business and was looking for a way to get out without losing too much money.

He said, "I paid too much for it originally and have never been able to catch up with the constantly-growing outstanding interest payments. I feel as if I have a noose around my neck and it is choking me every day."

Of course he could not discuss this issue with any of his staff and was even hesitant to mention the problem to his wife. He hinted that he felt like a failure. He said he was paralyzed by anxiety and was so pleased to get some of this worry off his chest by having someone to talk to.

I asked, "What are some of your options?"

He listed a few. All of them were tainted with the idea of escaping the pain.

Then I asked, "What would happen if some other printing company wanted to expand and was looking for additional capacity and maybe even a sniff of your client base?"

All of a sudden the air of negativity lifted and he could see the possibility of allying his business with someone else – perhaps participating in a larger scenario with partners who might be better-suited to this kind of business than he was.

His whole demeanor changed radically in a split second as the AHA effect clothed his mind with this chink of light in the fog that had enveloped him.

He began to speak more quickly and there was a new excitement in his voice.

We cut the call short because he wanted to dive into researching this possibility immediately.

Over the next few days he tackled this new approach and has come up with four fresh possibilities to take his business to the next step.

AHA Moments...

- Let's see our clients as they could be at their very best, rather than as they are now.

- Let's commit ourselves to ensure every coaching session makes a difference in our clients' lives.

24

Tune-in to Our Inner Voice

There are so many books, CD's, references and downloads on the Internet about business and psychology that we've become walking encyclopedias on most topics in these areas and probably have the answers to most problems in our heads. All we have to do is tap into this vast resource, called 'Our Inner Voice,' and pop-out the answers we need.

If the answers are there, why don't we access them? One reason is we do not know the questions. That's why we need a coach to probe and clarify what is bothering us or what is missing.

Thousands of business people tell me they wake-up early most mornings, between 4 AM and 5 AM, with their minds churning over challenging issues that need resolution or are bothering them. They also tell me that many answers pop-up during these times and result in practical actions taken.

Somehow when the mind is quiet, our inner voice talks and tells us what to do. Many business people say these answers are more valuable than most advice they receive from others.

- Have you had this experience?

- Do you regularly access your inner voice?

- Do you trust your judgment or do you need a supposed genius to help you make these critical decisions?

It is our personal encyclopedia of vast, practical knowledge, but seldom used.

What a waste!

Let's try it by heightening our awareness when these moments appear and test our judgment.

When I started my initial business my first obligation was to acquire some capital to ensure that I had an office and basic equipment in order to function effectively. Many nights I wrestled with the problem until one early morning it suddenly became clear. I needed to obtain a second mortgage on my home. At that moment I knew I was totally committed to my new business and was ready to take the risk of placing my home on the line to have the freedom of owning my own business.

Within days the money was in our bank account and we were ready to launch this important phase in our lives. It was scary, but the vision of being totally committed to my dream was clear.

The first couple of years were tough, but slowly we were able to generate sufficient revenue to justify the initial insight and ultimately the company became highly profitable.

The point was that the decision to take the plunge and leverage our major asset was made by me, alone one early morning, while half-asleep, based on accessing my intuition. Later, of course, I discussed the intention with my wife and key colleagues.

This was a significant step in my life and eased future challenges that beset me, all of which made me stronger and more adept at being in business.

Jane L.'s passion is fashion. After graduation from college, with a marketing degree, she went to work for a large department store. Finding that culture too restrictive she changed jobs and became a buyer, and in charge of the advertising, for a nationwide chain of 30 upscale boutiques.

Now, after five years, Jane wants to start her own boutique, but she's never done anything on her own and is terrified of all she needs to do and doesn't know where to star. Jane and I discussed her vision.

I asked, "What does your inner voice tell you about how this business looks?"

She told me and then she documented her vision, clearly, in short sentences in the present tense, one idea at a time.

Then I asked, "So now, how do you feel about this picture? Is it real for you? Would you go through the pain of making it happen knowing the risk you are about to take?"

She was so excited and started to talk with enthusiasm and genuine optimism – almost as though a huge barrier had been removed from her path.

"It's so clear now!" she said, "I can do this."

For me it was very satisfying to participate in this AHA experience, knowing that with a few choice questions, I had helped Jane verbalize and document the direction of her whole new life.

We are currently working on the details and the modus operandi. It's on the way and it will work because it is clear and doable. Prior to our dialogue this was just a 'child' dreaming, but never believing it was possible. This was not my agenda speaking, it was hers. I was simply the coach that caused it!

AHA Moments...

- Let's stretch ourselves to find the right questions.

- If the answers are there, let's access them?

- A coach should probe and clarify what is bothering the client.

25

Dialogue not just Discussion

dis·cus·sion (n.) A formal discourse on a topic; an exposition

di·a·logue or di·a·log (n). An exchange of ideas or opinions

Most of our lives revolve around talking with people – sometimes talking at others – sometimes listening – sometimes it is a discussion and sometimes it is a dialogue.

These are completely different processes and in coaching we need to be patently aware of what we are aiming to achieve.

Professional coaching embraces 'dialogue' more than 'discussion.' Adult to adult dialogue keeps us from falling into the trap of talking down to clients as though they are inferior. A humanistic mindset dialogue draws the best from clients because they feel free to be creative without fear of making fools of themselves. They can test themselves being their very best in an adult to adult dialogue.

If you are aware of the language I am using to write this book, notice my constant emphasis on the word 'we' as opposed to 'you.'

Virtually nothing bothers me more than self-appointed gurus who believe they have just descended from Mount Zion and have all the answers to the world's ills. Moreover they communicate as though they have resolved all their issues, but we mere mortals need guidance and help to attain their lofty levels. The reality is that most of these self-appointed, ego-driven gurus are every bit as fragile, frightened and imperfect as anyone else in the world and most are in desperate need of support. That is why they define themselves in these terms in order to demand huge dollops of recognition. Without constant applause most of them would shrivel up and die.

Most of these people define themselves by how they are thought of by others. They have insatiable approval needs instead of setting their own goals and measuring their value against their own standards. This is called 'living up to our own highest standards,' not the standards of others.

Do you know people who constantly demand attention and if they are not the focus of attention, create some diversion to maintain the focus on themselves? They talk about themselves incessantly and when we respond by offering our opinions or try to create a dialogue they visibly switch off until the light is back on them again. Then their energy level increases once more as our energy diminishes. These thinking styles drain the momentum of people and block meaningful communication.

Let's become aware of sharing our energy in a balanced manner with others. Let our communication become a win-win process through meaningful adult-to-adult dialogue.

AHA Moments...

- As professionals, let's embrace 'dialogue' more than 'discussion.'

- Let's speak the language of adult to adult dialogue to keep from falling into the trap of talking down to others as though they are inferior.

- Take note of the language I have used to write this book. Notice my constant emphasis on the word 'we' as opposed to 'you' and the phrase, 'let's'...

What we verbalize or document becomes our reality.

Terry Ostrowiak

26

Let Action Live on the Tongue

Most days I feel as if I am surrounded by people who feel as if the world is going down the tubes. I have lived for some length of time in four different countries and worked in at least 26 diverse lands over a period of 40 years.

It doesn't make much difference where I have been. Most people talk about the same things. Mostly about stuff that is bothering them, or may bother them, and yet day after day they get by with relatively little suffering, sometimes a smattering of pain or inconvenience, but generally many of the things that worry us never happen.

The point is that as we verbalize these negative thoughts, we immediately deplete our energy level and become less able to focus on the moment and certainly not on the future. How can we run a successful business when we are constantly looking back at the stupid mistakes we made, rather than focusing on the possibilities coming up in the future?

I am not suggesting we ignore the negatives, mistakes or challenges we face, just put them in perspective, resolve them as quickly as possible and move forward.

One of the most irritating questions I hear people asking is: "Why did you do that...?" referring to some irrational action I may have taken. All that query achieves is to yank us back into a past failure experience, suck out our energy and prevent us from moving forward to design our future the way we want it to take shape. No wonder we can't self-actualize. Our so-called friends or colleagues just pull us back to their miserable reality.

The next time someone says: "Why did you do that?" Answer: "I learned and have moved forward." Or ignore the question and ask: "What's next on our agenda?"

Another possibility is that our so-called friends or colleagues are simply enemies trying to suck out our energy and subconsciously want to bring us down to their level.

Stay away from them. Ask yourself: "Do I feel stronger and more energetic with certain people around me, or do I feel drained after being with some individuals?"

If we sensitively tune into our inner-voice and ask ourselves these questions each time we meet people, we may suddenly have the answer as to why we are depressed sometimes or ecstatic at other times.

In the film *Little Miss Sunshine,* Olive asks her Grandpa:

"Am I a loser?"

He asks, "Whatever gave you that idea?"

She replies, "My Dad hates losers."

He gently and lovingly says, "You are not a loser. Only people who stop trying are losers and you haven't stopped trying, have you? You are the most beautiful person in the world."

She asks, "Really? You're just saying that."

He says, "Really!"

She smiles with satisfaction.

What an AHA moment!

An instant transformation! With a few chosen words, she is moved from 'Impossibility to Certainty'.

Great coaching!

Let's manage our lives more intentionally instead of becoming victims of others' yoyo moods. This small adjustment in behavior could make a huge difference in our performance at work and home.

'What we say and how we say it' to our families, our staff, our clients and our colleagues, shapes the direction we take and influences all other stakeholders too.

AHA Moments...

- When we verbalize negative thoughts, we immediately deplete our energy level and become less able to focus.

- Let's manage our lives more intentionally instead of becoming victims of others' yoyo moods.

- Remember, 'What we say and how we say it' to our families, our staff, our clients and our colleagues, shapes the direction we take and influences all our stakeholders.

27

Make it Easy to Do

Create context around the learning so that everything is relevant.

When people are in trouble or suffering from stress or are under pressure, they tend to exaggerate the situation they are in and can't see the picture from a helicopter view. They are often subjective and unable to find rational solutions to the problems they face.

If highly skilled coaches listen intuitively to issues, they can unravel the mystery for their clients by playing the role of an objective sounding board. Because they are not emotionally involved they see the challenges objectively and can ask the right questions to lead the client to meaningful solutions.

Vincent B., a client, called this weekend and asked for assistance. He suddenly realized he was swamped with things to do and was trying to be the CEO and COO at the same time. It's a business and trying to fulfill two different functions simultaneously was always going to be difficult.

I asked, "Who can relieve you of some of these functions?"

He said, "My financial guy is doing a good job, but he's new and hasn't got much management background."

We agreed he would have his financial guy complete some profiles and I could talk with him to assess what he needed to take over in Operating Functions. This would be valuable for both of them. The new man would grow from the challenge and Vincent would have more time to focus on strategy instead of being too busy to get anything accomplished.

Vincent didn't see this possibility at first, but by having someone to talk to who encouraged him to listen to his inner-voice, the solution just popped up naturally at the appropriate moment.

Counselors listen well. Coaches, on the other hand, because they always work on the clients' agenda, not their own, 'make it easy to do by quickly getting the client into action'.

AHA Moments...

- Listen intuitively to issues, and unravel the mystery for our clients by playing the role of an objective sounding board.

- Ask the right questions to lead the client to meaningful solutions. Because we are not emotionally involved we can see the challenges objectively.

- Make it easier to do by quickly getting the client into action'.

Nothing is as far away as one minute ago.

JIM BISHOP

28

Create Urgency to Get Things Done

While coaching and training over the years, I discovered that both pace and energy are important elements in learning.

If coaches and trainers slow down the learning process, learners find their minds wandering and are not as focused as they were when the speed of the process is increased.

One of the characteristics I always look for in coaches is a natural energy level that injects urgency into learning situations. Of course we can all consciously speed up the process, but if it is a natural part of the coaches' repertoire it can be naturally energetic without putting on a façade for the occasion.

On the other hand coaches who tend to be more cerebral or rational focus on specifics and getting things right rather than on creating a personalized, emotional impact. They are probably better suited to technical or system coaching.

Melanie E. was an excellent student trained to be a coach and a delight to work with as she soaked up everything she was taught.

She was always willing to try something new and everyone loved her. When she instructed, she was always clear and systematic.

The only problem was that she missed nuances in her relationship with clients and was slightly off-track at reading between the lines of what was really going on under the surface of the dialogue. One of the reasons for this miscommunication was that she was too focused on her own agenda and getting it right, rather than focusing on the client's agenda and adapting her perspective to what the client wanted.

As a result of this difference in 'thinking styles' she decided to take up a lecturing post at a local university and was extremely happy to have made the switch. Ultimately, she was far better suited to university communication styles than the free-flowing, person-centered coaching methods we were implementing.

AHA Moments...

- Let's coach with a sense of urgency to keep the dialogue focused on results

- Maintain our positive energy throughout each session because it is contagious and rubs off on the client.

29

We Learn From Or Failures, but Grow From Our Successes

In a coaching session recently with a businessman, my client related a series of incidents from his past. At various times he had been emotionally hurt by remarks from people close to him. Sometimes it was his parents. Sometimes his wife and sometimes remarks made by colleagues.

It was very apparent that he was lugging around this baggage. Day after day he collected stories to prove how unfortunate he had been in his life. He was so focused on these failed experiences that he was literally unable to see any joy in the future.

In fact, when he was enjoying some pleasurable experience he would immediately check himself with these negative past failures. It was almost as though he was not permitted to let go of them and allow himself to participate with wild abandon in the fun of the moment.

Somehow he had learned to be supremely cautious about the adage, "We learn from our failures." He was told many times: "Do not…"

Being a good boy from a good background and being mainly cooperative and helpful, he took these instructions to heart and always obeyed them.

He had also learned to play down his successes – to be modest, not boastful. Nothing wrong with that attitude, except that he could not even quietly give himself credit for things he did well.

As a teenager, I remember reading a story from Readers' Digest about a small boy who went out one weekend with his grandfather to shoot pheasant in the swamps. With his first shot he managed to bring down one bird. He was ecstatic and the praise from his grandfather was even more pleasurable.

However, from then on, he was unable to reproduce the initial success. The more he failed the more despondent he became until he was just a bag of misery with a rifle.

The grandfather, seeing what was happening, decided to break the pattern of misery and said to the child: "Picture the first shot. Remember how you felt. Feel the trigger as you did the first time today and then squeeze."

The boy did what he was told. Surprise, surprise the next shot was successful.

I was playing in the final of my Tennis Club Championships a few weeks after reading this story and decided to implement what I had learned from it.

Whenever I had an important point to play in the match, I would visualize myself playing a chosen shot, perfectly, as I had done previously in the game.

I was amazed at the positive results I achieved and vowed to make this strategy an important part of my repertoire forever in sport, public speaking, coaching or any challenging situation I had to face in the future.

It wasn't just the visualization portion that made a difference for me. It was the way I started to walk and breathe – the lightness of being that suddenly enveloped me as I pictured myself hitting the shot perfectly.

Nowadays, when I play golf I do the same thing. I consciously remind myself and consciously picture the event of hitting the perfect shot as I had done earlier.

The more I discipline myself to create this 'positive addiction' the more I can perform at an optimum level in any sphere of my life where excelling is vital to the result.

Bottom line, I always create a model for myself, performing excellently, as a guide for success, based on the principle: 'We grow from our successes.'

It has always worked wonders for me. Maybe it will work for you too? Try it!

AHA Moments...

- Learn from our failures.
- Grow from our successes.
- Create a model for ourselves, performing excellently.

30

Conclude Each Session by Reinforcing New Learning

In the to-and-fro of dialogue, we become so mentally and emotionally involved in the process that we often forget some of the things we covered earlier in the conversation. Many times these are vital AHA moments, but are lost when our minds are jerked into new directions.

It is vital for the client to document the insight immediately. ***I encourage all my clients to keep a running journal of the things we discuss and to list AHAs on the last page for easy reference.*** After all, the value of the dialogue rests completely on these moments. They are like the nuggets saved from the fire and long after the conversation has been forgotten, the AHAs live on and remind us of a previous, vital moment in our evolvement.

In summary, always review the insights gleaned by asking the client to:

- Verbalize the answer to the question: "What did you discover about yourself?"

- Explain why each insight is important and wait for an answer.

- Tell what they are going to do differently as a result of this discovery or rediscovery.

- Think about possible barriers preventing implementation.

- Work out how to overcome the barrier.

- Finally, outline a benefit they would receive from completing this new project, to reinforce it.

This question process ensures that we leave the client with a clear plan and direction for the following few days. It is the essence of what we included in our dialogue so they feel totally in control of managing their own agenda.

When we follow up in the next session we can easily attach a thread to the previous meeting by asking: "What resulted from our last discussion?"

This means we are continually reinforcing the client's agenda and building on it in a very personal way.

AHA Moments...

- Encourage clients to keep a running journal of the things discussed and to list AHA moments on the last page of their journal for easy reference.

- Strive to achieve at least one AHA moment in each coaching session.

- Leave the client with a clear plan and direction to follow.

- Make it clear that there will be follow-up questions at the next session to reinforce commitment.

- Reinforcing new learning makes it concrete and doable and ensures it becomes reality.

When someone shows you who they are, believe them.

MAYA ANGELOU

31

Heighten Our Awareness of 'The Pygmalion Effect'

Belief in potential creates potential.

If you tell a grammar school classroom teacher a child is bright, the teacher will be more supportive, teach more difficult material, allow more time to answer questions, and provide more feedback to that child. The child receiving this attention and basking in the teacher's belief learns more and does better in school. It does not matter if the child is actually bright. All that matters is that the teacher believes in the child. This is also true of managers and workers.

This uniquely human phenomenon is called the Pygmalion Effect. It is a persistently held belief in another person such that the belief becomes a reality. The person believed in, being believed, becomes the person whom they are perceived to be: the self fulfilling prophecy.

Did you ever notice there are some people with whom we naturally feel comfortable? Who think our ideas are great. When they listen to us, we express ourselves clearly and are able to make ideas ring with clarity and insight. This is because, believing we are bright, they see us in this light. Knowing how they feel about us, we work hard to make sure they are satisfied with our answers.

The opposite is also true. There are people with whom we are not comfortable and who we believe do not like us. We avoid these people and do not do our best when we are around them. With these people we are hesitant and much less articulate. We are less likely to try hard to get them to understand our point of view. We are victims of a label placed on us by another.

What the Research Says

This is also true in the supervisor/employee relationship. Researchers looked at 12 separate research studies from different work settings, involving a total of 2,874 participants using a technique called meta analysis. All studies involved employees and their supervisor (the person who was responsible to oversee and evaluate their work). Each study randomly assigned employees to two groups and supervisors were told that one group of employees had considerably greater potential than the other group. Thus, a positive attitude was fostered on the part of supervisors about one group of employees who were basically no different from the other group.

With only two exceptions employees in the groups about whom the supervisors were given positive information responded with greater productivity. The magnitude of these gains seemed to be dependent on the circumstances of the work relationship. The greatest gains were seen in military training settings. The researchers suspect this is because in the military it is easier to control the information supervisors receive, whereas, in a business situation word of mouth and reputation may bleed into the situation making the information received by the supervisor less believable.

However, looking at findings in elementary school settings there seems to be something that happens in a learning situation that is different from what happens in a work situation. It is possible that a positive attitude on the part of supervisors may have a greater effect on learning than it does on work productivity.

The second greatest gains were found in the situations where disadvantaged workers (those who, for whatever reason, were less likely to be successful) were randomly assigned to two groups. The group about whom the supervisor was given positive information made significant gains over the group about whom the supervisor was not given positive information. It is suspected people with low self-esteem and self-efficacy are more likely to respond to positive feedback. This indicates that supervisors have the potential to create high performing employees. All that is needed is for them to believe the employee has potential, the Pygmalion Effect. This is probably because the employee is more fully engaged and motivated when working for a positive thinking supervisor, allowing the organization to fully tap into his or her capabilities.

Fewer gains resulted when supervisors had less chance to be with subordinates, such as in a sales situation when employees work independently and away from the supervisor. Women supervisors were less likely to be affected by the Pygmalion Effect. It was observed that women, regardless of their beliefs, seemed to treat employees equally. Therefore, the group of employees about whom a women supervisor was given positive information made less significant gains over the other group. This was even truer when the supervisor and all the employees were women.

The Pygmalion Effect is an important key to creating or improving performance. Everything should be done to create a highly positive attitude about employees in the minds of their bosses, and employees should feel that their bosses and the business believe in their potential as people.

Donald Y. is a natural handyman – that's what he does for a living. His business is good and customers are all either repeat or word-of-mouth referrals. Business is going so well that Donald has no time for anything else. He works seven days a week, 10-12 hour days. Donald brought in two assistants (employees) about a year ago. However, Donald is used to doing everything himself and it's been very difficult for him to let his two assistants assume control of any job. Donald is always looking over their shoulders because he 'knows' no one can do the job as well as he does.

This was a typical scenario of 'Superman' at work with his highly overpaid staff watching him perform. When not performing he was hassling them as they tried to live up to his awesome reputation – or so he thought. The ilk of Ayatollah bosses in small or even large businesses is a scourge for achieving sustainable results. Not only that, but they make people's lives a misery as they stomp around in the limelight driven by anguished insecurity, expressed by benevolent power and intolerance.

I asked Donald, "What do you do best in your company, love doing and spend a great deal of time doing?"

He told me he was a master craftsman and he desperately wanted to offload some of the responsibility he was carrying, but frankly did not have enough confidence in his two assistants to let them become fully accountable for the standards and results he wanted them to achieve.

I asked, "Do you ever take them with you on a job to watch you work and explain what it is that you do so well?"

He replied, "No!"

He had done that initially, but later let them work unsupervised. He agreed that he was very critical and generally dissatisfied with their work, but had done little to resolve the problem other than to quietly express his irritation to others about their performance which he saw as blight on his reputation.

I asked him to read 'The Pygmalion Effect' in order to see his assistants in a more positive light. Then I suggested he ask each of them to take over one of his favorite projects and ask them to commit to producing a result they would be ecstatic about achieving for themselves – never mind their customers.

Then I suggested, "Try saying this to your assistants: 'I am proud to work with you because I know what excellent work you are capable of producing.' "

I had to coach him on the exercise because it did not seem real for him, but he recognized how vital this project was for his business and how it would be a turning point in his career.

It worked! His assistants were at first somewhat skeptical, but accepted the challenge and achieved the results Donald had visualized and transferred to them.

From that moment on he knew what to do to expand his business by growing his people. At first he challenged them to live up to 'His Highest Expectations', and then challenged them to live up to 'Their Own Highest Expectations'.

He was amazed at their response and even more surprised by his ability to flexibly change his style of behavior.

Obviously this was a significant achievement and a good example of the Pygmalion Effect in action. It's also important to understand none of this would have occurred without an experienced coach to create the new possibility.

AHA Moments...

- Let's remember: "Our belief in the potential of others creates their reality."

- Initially, let's challenge our clients to live up to our 'highest expectations' and then.

- Challenge them to live up to 'their own highest expectations'.

32

Live up to High Expectations

How do we know what our own Highest Expectations should be? Just as important in small or large business is knowing precisely what is expected from us and from others. The answer is most of the time we have no idea what is expected from us and, more importantly, we often don't have a clue what we should expect from ourselves or others.

The reason is we have never asked the right questions to elicit the correct responses.

So we drift along guessing what we should be doing in the job or what is expected from us. Generally, the only time we really get helpful feedback is when we screw-up and, in desperation, someone tells us the true status of our performance – mainly negative criticism. This means, when 'someone' wants to talk to us, we know we are in trouble. Mostly they don't tell us when we are doing well because doing well is what is expected of us - so why bother?

If we are serious about our careers and genuinely want to grow and succeed, what follows is an idea I have tested with a number of my clients and it has worked magnificently in almost every situation.

Live up to others' Highest Expectations, initially.

Let's go to someone whose opinion counts and who cares about us and say: "If I were to be doing an outstanding job, what would you expect of me?" Then say: "Please do not give me an answer immediately. You may have to think about it so it has total relevance for me."

This is what I mean about accessing our intuition. In this case we access their intuition, ask them to document their thoughts and communicate it to us. What happens is we are now on the same wavelength as those people and know exactly what they believe is 'us at our best'.

Now we have something worthwhile to strive for and it's a great reason to grow and develop.

Then, live up to our own Highest Expectations

Let's sit down and write a vision statement, just for ourselves for the next twenty years. Now refine it to ten years, five years and one year. Let's access our intuition and document it as a blueprint for our future. The chances are we will subconsciously attain something pretty close to the picture in our mind and we can always make subtle or even big changes as we progress. At least we obviate the general trend of just going with the flow and suddenly waking up one day and asking: "What am I doing here? This is not where I wanted to be!"

I met a young man in Chicago a number of years ago who told me he was an actor. Part- time he worked as a doorman at an hotel because it was quite profitable. He did this for a number of years and slowly became more comfortable being a doorman and did less acting.

I asked him, "Are you an actor working part-time as a doorman or a doorman who occasionally acts?"

These questions shook him to the core. He was stunned when he realized how he had submissively slipped into the comfort zone and was never going to fulfill his dream of becoming a professional actor. His dream had faded away and he could no longer say he was an actor. He was just a doorman carrying bags and directing traffic in and out of the hotel. Nothing wrong with being a doorman, but I knew he wanted much more than just working in a menial job. He wanted to exploit his dramatic skills and write scripts. Now he had settled for less.

Within a few weeks he did a thinking-style profile with me, moved to Los Angeles and found a job with a top TV studio.

He writes scripts and has initiated an experimental theater group who meet regularly.

It was a tough move away from the comfort of his primary occupation, but now he has dignity and exploits his creativity to be able to reach his life's purpose.

Charles Handy, a futurist from the UK, wrote a piece I will never forget in his book *The Age of Unreason*.

He said: "If you place a frog in a pot of water on a stove and heat it, the frog will slowly boil and die as it adjusts to the minute increases in temperature."

How many human beings adjust to more and more discomfort until it is too late to move? They literally die because they adapted themselves to the creeping pain rather than take a chance and look for a new opportunity. Their fear of confronting unacceptable situations is greater than losing the piece of security they crave.

The value of our lives is determined by discovering as quickly as possible what we are best-suited for, love, or are passionate about, and then pursuing our dream until we transform it from 'Possibility to Certainty'.

Recently I was on a flight into Los Angeles from Amsterdam and sitting across the aisle from me was Paul Verhoeven, a world-renowned Hollywood and European Film Director.

I asked him how he got into filmmaking and he said: "I started off as a mathematician and during my military service I found myself taking pictures and filming for the division I was serving. Soon after, I realized clearly that my future lay in making films rather than mathematics." He could so easily have gone the other way, but his instinct guided him and he followed it to become the international success he is today.

Sometimes we know what we have to do with our lives. Sometimes the talent or skill appears so vividly we cannot avoid doing what is so obvious. Most of us, however, have to dig deeply to discover what it is we really want to achieve in our lifetime. This is why we need to become adept at accessing our intuition, interpreting it correctly and then, vitally, documenting it to ensure it is clear.

This is how most people go into business, small or large or even home-based. We are driven by our intuition, not logic. Often deciding to start a business is totally irrational, but the drive to own our own businesses is so strong it even overrides common sense at times. Strong drive, often called passion, carries us through the hurdles, challenges and bad times and we suddenly wake-up one day and know "We have done it! We can make it work! We can fulfill our dreams!"

AHA Moments...

- Live up to others' Highest Expectations, initially.

- Then, live up to our own Highest Expectations.

- The value of our lives is determined by discovering as quickly as possible what we are best-suited for, love, or are passionate about and then pursuing our dream until we transform it from 'Possibility to Certainty'.

If we concentrate on finding whatever is good in every situation, we discover that our lives are suddenly filled with gratitude – a feeling that nurtures the soul.

Rabbi Harold Kushner

33

Remembering Names

Twelve of us had just finished up our usual weekly golf game one Saturday and were having lunch in the club dining room. One of the waiters had mixed-up an order and a fairly new member commented – almost proudly, "Most of the waiters here don't know my name!" He continued to shake his head, as if saying to himself: "What do you expect from these people?"

I could not help but ask quietly, "How many of their names do you know?"

Now there was silence at the table with this apparent mild confrontation. All the golfers were focused on him, waiting for his reply.

Embarrassed now at being in the limelight, he blurted out, "Why should I bother to learn them? I'm in computers. All of you are in business, marketing or sales where it may be important, but in my field, it isn't."

One of the elder, white-haired players said, "All the staff here know my name and I know theirs. I make a point of it. We spend a lot of time here together!" – indicating that this is an extension of his home.

He continued, "How do you expect them to care about you, if you don't care about them?"

We all hear people say: "I remember faces, but not names!"

What a cop-out for not taking the time away from themselves for a moment.

During my second month of college, our professor gave us a pop quiz. I was a conscientious student and had breezed through the questions until I read the last one: what is the first name of the woman who cleans the school?"

Surely this was some kind of joke. I had seen the cleaning woman several times. She was tall, dark-haired and in her 50's, but how would I know her name?

I handed in my paper, leaving the last question blank. Just before class ended, one student asked if the last question would count toward our quiz grade.

"Absolutely" said the professor. "In your careers you will meet many people. All are significant. They deserve your attention and care, even if all you do is smile and say "hello."

I've never forgotten that lesson. I also learned her name was Dorothy.

A number of years ago I was conducting a workshop on remembering names for a class of 35 accountants and auditors in the Netherlands.

Suddenly, one of the participants, Frank K stood up and said,

"We've spent the last 20 minutes remembering names. What a waste of time! Most people we see briefly and maybe never again. Why take the trouble to do this? It's simply a waste of time and energy."

Of course I was stunned to be confronted so bluntly like this in front of 35 professionals in what had been an extremely positive exercise. The atmosphere immediately collapsed like a limp balloon. I felt I had to respond with some powerful impact and spluttered how important the concept of remembering names is in our society and how poorly we do this.

The group listened intently to my answer – probably thought 'I didn't get the point.' We quickly summarized the value of the session and then we stopped for the coffee break.

Here is the answer I would like to have given, but didn't.

One of the finest ways to develop self-confidence is to remember names.

The sheer act of taking the focus off ourselves for a moment and concentrating on the other person while listening carefully to them enunciating their names means we have taken the focus off of ourselves, felt less pressure and are free to interact with the speaker.

Normally when we are introducing ourselves or being introduced to others, we may feel slightly self-conscious, depending on our level of self-confidence. In order to remember names, we have to consciously think about the other person. So the more we focus on others, the less self-conscious we feel.

This means there is a direct correlation between remembering names and our level of self-confidence. The opposite is also true. Our inability to remember names in the moment is a direct reflection of our level of self-consciousness.

Thoughts that may run through our mind are:

- Will he/she like me?

- What kind of impression am I making?

- Will they notice some blemish that's bothering me? – and other distractions.

To have any chance of remembering names we have to banish these thoughts from our mind and fully concentrate on the other person and what they are saying.

Most times we don't even hear the name because we are so caught up in our own agenda, so what chance do we have of remembering it.

As silly as this regular, basic interaction seems, it is a good indicator of our level of professionalism and more importantly a good measure of our care for others whoever they may be.

Unfortunately, in that workshop, it was not possible to get into the depth required for a comprehensive, meaningful answer, but I was able to inject some of this background into further sessions.

A few days later, a friend of mine, Dr. Peter Robertson, a psychiatrist by profession, but also a management consultant in the company, explained to me how normal that remark is in The Netherlands.

People, he said do not automatically accept ideas, concepts, opinions or arguments from others without question. He went on to explain that kids in school, as part of their culture, are taught to think for themselves and question everything that is not self-evident. This is probably a throw-back from World War II where their neighbors were blindly led by authoritarian heads of government who ultimately took over their country as well.

He advised me, in similar situations in future, to not argue the point, just ask others in the group if they felt the same way and encourage them to express their opinions without judgment. In other words, acknowledge their right to say what they believe.

In our English speaking culture, we feel a need 'to win the argument' very much like a parent talking to a child.

Dutch Culture is more of an adult-to-adult communication – no judgment or dogma.

This is why Dutch executives and managers are always in meetings and their parliamentary system is one of proportional representation with many parties in the system and virtually every government is run by a coalition.

It's all a part of a culture of acknowledging the right of each person to be heard and they call this 'Relativering' or 'putting things in perspective' or 'looking at things from both sides – not just our opinion.'

AHA Moments...

- This is one of the pieces of the lubrication process in the moving parts of human relationships that reduces friction.

- Let's just take a few moments to listen carefully to the name and focus on others – not so much on us.

- Check out the Chapter on Cultural Differences as it adds value to our grasp of what is required of us to become universally adept in communicating sensitively to our changing world.

34

Demonstrating Leadership

Recently, I started to work with LO, the Marketing Director of an International Computer-based Company. She was a client of mine many years before and periodically called me into the company to do specific workshops and team assignments. This one was specifically coaching-oriented.

She admitted she was intimidated by her boss and periodically suffered real fear, jeopardizing her career. Although she is known as a tough cookie with her colleagues, she felt she was not functioning optimally.

Her first challenge was to understand her fear and to admit that her boss was extremely demanding of her and the management team to the extent that they were all afraid to be themselves in his presence. His attitude had led to mistakes and hesitancy, exacerbating and reinforcing any weaknesses in his group. As part of her coaching process, I challenged her to confront him positively about this issue so he would see her approach as a great compliment, not take offense and willingly act on her suggestion for change.

Just our mere dialogue diminished her fear and almost instantly she started to see him in a more positive light and appreciate his

Leadership, intellect and drive. She approached her boss, made him aware of the fear he instilled in the team and asked for his assistance in changing the atmosphere. It worked. She took the plunge and he responded wonderfully.

From this conversation, she eased her anxiety and started to see the exercise as a truly helpful growth experience turning it into a Quantum Leap experience for her and for the ongoing performance of her boss. She saw what a huge difference this new attitude injected into the whole organization and acknowledged she was the Catalyst causing the change.

So in the end, it was not just overcoming her initial anxiety, but an opportunity to positively affect the whole team's bottom-line results.

She also enrolled her marketing Team in the new approach, coached them to create a broader Vision for their division and persuaded them to continue to take full responsibility for their actions.

AHA Moment...

- By willingly sticking out our necks and taking a chance to demonstrate Leadership, we can overcome fear and perform even more effectively which could positively affect bottom-line results.

35

Performance Appraisals for Adults

In dealing with larger organizations I discovered that most managers dreaded appraisal meetings with their staff. This came about because managers were conditioned into believing that appraisals were meant to be a review of past performance especially mistakes made in the past as well as a guide for future bonuses and promotions.

With that perspective in mind obviously the appraisal meeting most often focuses on the failures of the employee in the past. No wonder both managers and staff, dread these meetings, often leaving the discussion with negative feelings about themselves, about their bosses and about the company. So the very positive expectation of value from the appraisal meeting is trashed and causes lowering of energy and feelings of disloyalty rather than enthusiasm for the future and the feeling of being part of a winning team.

DW discussed this process with me and he decided to approach it from a completely different viewpoint.

To create a more positive environment for these discussions he started to do the following:

1. He asked his staff to set the dates and times for these meetings instead of imposing that decision on them

2. He asked them to create the agenda and lead the process themselves.

3. He asked them to bring updated documents with them as evidence of their performance so that that the discussions were factual, not based on hearsay or rumor.

4. He asked them to compare their performance against their original plan for that period and discussed with them what had worked and what needed change or improvement for the future.

5. The tone of the dialogue was always future-based so that it focused on the hope for better performance to come, not on past failures that could not be changed.

As a result of this more adult-to-adult approach towards his staff he found that they were taking on more responsibility instead of waiting for him to initiate action.

The result was greater buy-in by staff because they had initiated the planning of their own development and therefore took greater responsibility for the results they were achieving.

This style of management ultimately results in a more adult culture that frees people to take on greater responsibility and commitment to Quantum Leap Results rather than just perform tasks assigned by their managers.

AHA Moments...

- Performance appraisals can be exciting opportunities rather than fearful events causing huge anxiety for both appraiser and appraisee.

- Ensure the appraisee initiates the performance appraisal meeting.

- Make sure the agenda for the meeting is designed by the appraisee.

36

Can You Sleep When the Wind Blows?

This is a story which had a profound impact on my thinking. Years ago, a farmer owned land along the Atlantic seacoast. He constantly advertised for hired hands. Most people were reluctant to work on farms along the shoreline. They dreaded the awful storms that raged across the Atlantic, wreaking havoc on the buildings and crops.

As the farmer interviewed applicants for the job, he received a steady stream of refusals.

Finally, a short, thin man, well past middle age, approached the farmer. "Are you a good farm hand?" the farmer asked him.

"Well, I can sleep when the wind blows," answered the little man.

Although puzzled by this answer, the farmer, desperate for help, hired him. The little man worked well around the farm, busy from dawn to dusk and the farmer felt satisfied with the man's work.

Then one night the wind howled loudly in from offshore. Jumping out of bed, the farmer grabbed a lantern and rushed next door to the hired hand's sleeping quarters. He shook the little man and yelled, "Get up! A storm is coming! Tie things down before they blow away!"

The little man rolled over in bed and said firmly, "No sir. I told you, I can sleep when the wind blows."

Enraged by the response, the farmer was tempted to fire him on the spot. Instead, he hurried outside to prepare for the storm. To his amazement, he discovered that all of the haystacks had been covered with tarpaulins. The cows were in the barn, the chickens were in the coops, and the doors were barred. The shutters were tightly secured. Everything was tied down.

Nothing could blow away. The farmer then understood what his hired hand meant, so he returned to his bed to sleep while the wind blew.

AHA Moments...

- When we're prepared, spiritually, mentally and physically, we have nothing to fear.

- Can you sleep when the wind blows?

37

Some Life Lessons

Each of these stories has a message as do most events in our lives. As you read these stories, what do we learn from them?

Be a Human Being

One night, at 11:30 p.m., an older African American woman was standing on the side of an Alabama highway trying to endure a lashing rain storm. Her car had broken down and she desperately needed a ride. Soaking wet, she decided to flag down the next car.

A young white man stopped to help her, generally unheard of in those conflict-filled 1960's. The man took her to safety, helped her get assistance and put her into a taxicab.

She seemed to be in a big hurry, but wrote down his address and thanked him.

Seven days went by and a knock came on the man's door. To his surprise, a giant console color TV was delivered to his home. A special note was attached. It read:

Thank you so much for assisting me on the highway the other night. The rain drenched not only my clothes, but also my spirits.

Then you came along. Because of you, I was able to make it to my dying husband's bedside just before he passed away ... God bless you for helping me and unselfishly serving others."

Sincerely,

Mrs. Nat King Cole

Always Remember Those Who Serve

In the days when an ice cream sundae cost much less, a 10-year-old boy entered a hotel coffee shop and sat at a table. A waitress put a glass of water in front of him.

"How much is an ice cream sundae?" he asked.

"Fifty cents," replied the waitress.

The little boy pulled his hand out of his pocket and studied the coins in it.

"Well, how much is a plain dish of ice cream?" he inquired.

By now more people were waiting for a table and the waitress was growing impatient.

"Thirty-five cents," she brusquely replied.

The little boy again counted his coins.

"I'll have the plain ice cream," he said.

The waitress brought the ice cream, put the bill on the table and walked away. The boy finished the ice cream, paid the cashier and left. When the waitress came back, she began to cry as she wiped down the table. There, placed neatly beside the empty dish, were two nickels and five pennies.

You see, he couldn't have the sundae, because he had to have enough left to leave her a tip.

The Obstacle in Our Path

In ancient times, a King had a boulder placed on a roadway. Then he hid himself and watched to see if anyone would remove the huge rock. Some of the king's wealthiest merchants and courtiers came by and simply walked around it. Many loudly blamed the King for not keeping the roads clear, but none did anything about getting the stone out of the way.

Then a peasant came along carrying a load of vegetables. Upon approaching the boulder, the peasant laid down his burden and tried to move the stone to the side of the road. After much pushing and straining, he finally succeeded. After the peasant picked up his load of vegetables, he noticed a purse lying in the road where the boulder had been. The purse contained many gold coins and a note from the King indicating that the gold was for the person who removed the boulder from the roadway. The peasant learned what many of us never understand!

Every obstacle presents an opportunity to improve our condition.

Give When It Counts

Many years ago, when I worked as a volunteer at a hospital, I got to know a little girl named Liz who was suffering from a rare and serious disease. Her only chance of recovery appeared to be a blood transfusion from her 5-year old brother, who had miraculously survived the same disease and had developed the antibodies needed to combat the illness. The doctor explained the situation to her little brother, and asked the little boy if he would be willing to give his blood to his sister.

I saw him hesitate for only a moment before taking a deep breath and saying, "Yes I'll do it if it will save her."

As the transfusion progressed, he lay in bed next to his sister and smiled, as we all did, seeing the color returning to her cheek. Then his face grew pale and his smile faded.

He looked up at the doctor and asked with a trembling voice, "Will I start to die right away."

Being young, the little boy had misunderstood the doctor – he thought he was going to have to give his sister all his blood in order to save her.

38

AHA Moments List

The following is a listing of all the AHA Moments found in this book.

- Coaching means visualizing people at their very best, rather than as they are now.

- The vital distinction between consulting, mentoring, advising, instructing, and counseling vs. coaching is that the coach serves as a catalyst and focuses only on the client's agenda. Other disciplines are almost solely focused on their own professional agendas.

- Coaching is not meant to be a long-term process, but rather the right tool for the right moment

- Focus on others' achievements and struggles, not ours – a great way to develop more self-confidence.

- Challenge clients to open themselves to change.

- Create an adult to adult relationship.

- Straight talk with dialogue and deep respect is better than 'being nice' or being 'autocratic.

- Ask for Permission to coach in a Process of Willing Cooperation.

- Experience being coached by a skilled professional to understand the subtle nuances in coaching.

- Remember, coaching requires intricate, sensitive and superior communication skills to make it work optimally.

- Focus solely on the clients' need. Be flexible and devoid of ego.

- Ensure the trust level is beyond question for the Coaching Process to work optimally and truthfully.

- Coaching is a special relationship – certainly not for everyone.

- If coaches have to sell or strongly convince prospective clients to do business with them, the relationship will probably not work. Better let it go than force the issue.

- Unlike consulting, where the professionals come into a business, write plans and strategies, get paid and leave, coaching is an event-driven process.

- The coach agrees on specific, measurable targets to be achieved with their clients and then walks in step with them until the goal has been achieved

- As a professional coach, use profiles as a starting point in a coaching relationship – not as an end in itself.

- The objective of using profiles should be to create insights and smooth communication leading to more profitable results, not to be the total focus of the exercise.

- "Catch people doing things right and tell them".

- Comment on people's strength's. Reinforce those strengths and ensure they see themselves in a better light.

- Add energy and urgency to the client. This is the underlying base of all coaching

- Challenge clients to verbally create their future rather than focus on the static past. Greater energy and excitement result from the exercise.

- See clients as they could be, not as they are today.

- Communicate their potential to them again and again until it becomes their reality.

- Coach clients to access their intuition. This is not just an airy-fairy act, but an initial, vital piece of the puzzle in creating a concrete plan for a business.

- Encourage clients to visualize a concrete vision of the future for their businesses.

- Challenge clients to use clear word-pictures – not just conceptual language.

- Remember: The reality is that writing the plan is the second or third part of the process not the first.

- Recognize that all business owners face moments of doubt, feelings of inadequacy and/or fear of failure.

- Help clients to eliminate doubt by coaching them with intuitive questions.

- Challenge clients to constantly remind themselves to say: "I have the Power. I make the Decisions".

- Show genuine belief in our client's ability to change.

- Remind clients that change is never easy because people around us do not like us to change. It seems to upset their equilibrium.

- Coach our employees to find their own personal method to implement new ways of doing things within their own context, not the coach's context.

- Always be there as a friend, confidant, advisor and supporter

- Start with vision. Not goals. It's a simple process, but not always easy to implement.

- Coach clients to develop a clear vision that evokes their passion, then to write goals that reflect their deepest desires.

- Give clients the experience of 'being genuinely listened to'.

- Active Listening is accessing what is happening underneath the words, not necessarily what is initially being said on the surface.

- Take note that 'practice makes perfect' is probably true, but more relevant is – 'practice makes permanent'.

- 'Just do it' – the Nike Ad says. When we say: "I will try to…" it indicates we are expecting to fail and are simply creating an alibi to justify it.

- Find out what we are doing right and do it more often.

- Remember – 'We learn from our mistakes, but we grow from our successes'.

- Let's make sure that we are not just understood, but that we're not misunderstood.

- Remember that the high cost of correcting mistakes, in time and money, is a huge drain on our business.

- Ask our clients to write a plan based on their highest expectations.

- Challenge clients to achieve a goal far beyond anything they ever conceived of previously as being a possibility.

- Test this idea – "When we are early, we control the situation. When we are late or just on time, the situation controls us."

- Never forget – "Our credibility in any relationship is built on trust."

- English, Scandinavian, German, and Dutch speaking people of the world are distinctly monochronic – meaning that time is the defining value of their culture.

- Polychronic people such as French, Italian, Spanish and Portuguese speaking people, as well as people from Africa and The Middle East place more emphasis on relationships than on time as the defining value of their culture.

- Regardless of differences in culture, we need to be highly sensitive to the diverse ways people from other places process information and therefore respond.

- Ensure we never assume people from other areas, regions, or countries are the same as us.

- Neither children, teenagers or adults like to be 'talked at'. Let's speak and be spoken to as adults talking to adults.

- Let's stop giving solutions to problems – rather allow others to come up with their own solutions.

- Let's see our clients as they could be at their very best, rather than as they are now.

- Let's commit ourselves to ensure every coaching session makes a difference in our clients' lives.

- Let's stretch ourselves to find the right questions.

- If the answers are there, let's access them.

- A coach probes and clarifies what is bothering the client.

- As professionals, let's embrace 'dialogue' more than 'discussion'.

- Let's speak the language of adult to adult dialogue to keep from falling into the trap of talking down to others as though they are inferior.

- Take note of the language I have used to write this book. Notice my constant emphasis on the word 'we' as opposed to 'you' and the phrase, 'let's…

- When we verbalize negative thoughts, we immediately deplete our energy level and become less able to focus.

- Let's manage our lives more intentionally instead of becoming victims of others' yoyo moods.

- Remember, 'What we say and how we say it' to our families, our staff, our clients and our colleagues, shapes the direction we take and influences all our stakeholders.

- Listen intuitively to issues, and unravel the mystery for our clients by playing the role of an objective sounding board.

- Ask the right questions to lead the client to meaningful solutions. Because we are not emotionally involved we can see the challenges objectively.

- Make it easier to do by quickly getting the client into action.

- Let's coach with a sense of urgency to keep the dialogue focused on results.

- Maintain our positive energy throughout each session because it is contagious and rubs off on the client.

- Learn from our failures.

- Grow from our successes.

- Create a model for ourselves, performing excellently.

- Encourage clients to keep a running journal of the things discussed and to list AHA moments on the last page of their journal for easy reference.

- Strive to achieve at least one AHA moment in each coaching session.

- Leave the client with a clear plan and direction to follow.

- Make it clear that there will be follow-up questions at the next session to reinforce commitment.

- Let's remember: 'Our belief in the potential of others strengthens their reality.'

- Reinforcing new learning makes it concrete and do-able and ensures it becomes reality.

- Initially, let's challenge our clients to live up to our 'highest expectations' and then…

- Challenge them to live up to 'their own highest expectations'.

- The value of our lives is determined by discovering as quickly as possible what we are best-suited for, love, or are passionate about and then pursuing our dream until we transform it from 'Possibility to Certainty'.

- Remembering names is a piece of the lubrication process in the intricate moving parts of Human Relationships that reduces friction.

- Take a few brief moments to listen carefully to others and consciously focus on them as they mention their names.

- By willingly sticking out our necks and taking a chance to demonstrate Leadership, we can overcome fear and perform even more effectively which could positively affect bottom-line results.

- Life is not about winning at the expense of others.

- Life is about making sure people around us feel better about themselves as a result of being with us.

- When we're prepared, spiritually, mentally and physically, we have nothing to fear.

- By willingly sticking out our necks and taking a chance to demonstrate Leadership, we can overcome fear and perform even more effectively which could positively affect bottom-line results.

- Can you sleep when the wind blows?

- Performance appraisals can be exciting opportunities rather than fearful events causing huge anxiety for both appraiser and appraisee.

- Ensure the agenda for the meeting is designed by the appraisee.

The greatest discovery of my generation is that a human being can alter his life by altering his attitude of mind.

WILLIAM JAMES

AUTHOR'S NOTE

I specifically use the word 'Let's' and 'We' in coaching or training sessions as well as in my normal everyday discourse to demonstrate 'Adult to Adult' language not 'Parent to Child' language. It is gentle, non-threatening, polite, and respectful – but it is still a firm call for action with a sense of inclusiveness rather than a demand or command from me to you to do something. It also means I respect you. We have the same challenges. The message is: 'I am like you.'

For example: 'Let's go to town' instead of 'Go to town' which commands you to do it, but not me.

It says I am different. I am the messenger. I have superior status.

It's also patronizing. We are not inferior, we are not children and we are not in the army.

Let's all talk 'We Language'. We may find more adults rise to the fore around us as they live up to their own highest expectations; develop greater self-esteem and confidence while testing themselves in more challenging environments rather than wait for permission before they feel comfortable and ready to grow and develop.

Let's test it and see what happens!

Character is made by many acts. It can be lost by a single one.

ANONYMOUS

www.ingramcontent.com/pod-product-compliance
Lightning Source LLC
Chambersburg PA
CBHW020459030426
42337CB00011B/165